WITNESSING TOGETHER:

Forty Years of Ecumenical Theological Pilgrimage

WITNESSING TOGETHER:

Forty Years of Ecumenical Theological Pilgrimage

(Ruby Jubilee Publication)

Edited by
Fr. Dr. Jose John

Federated Faculty for
Research in Religion and Culture (FFRRC)
2022

WITNESSING TOGETHER: ***Forty Years of Ecumenical Theological Pilgrimage*** - Jointly Published by the Indian Society for Promoting Christian Knowledge (ISPCK), Post Box 1585, 1654, Madarsa Road, Kashmere Gate, Delhi-110006 and Federated Faculty for Research in Religion and Culture (FFRRC) C/O Mar Thoma Theological Seminary, P.B.287, Kottayam-686001 Kerala.

Online Order: http://ispck.org.in/book.php

Also available on amazon.in

ISBN: 978-93-90569-28-1

Laser typeset by

ISPCK, Post Box 1585, 1654, Madarsa Road, Kashmere Gate, Delhi-110006
• *Tel:* 23866323/22

e-mail: ashish@ispck.org.in • ella@ispck.org.in
website: www.ispck.org.in

Contents

Editorial board

Foreword

Questions Galore, Answers Sparse: Changing Context of Christian Mission and Ministry

Fr. Dr. K.M. George

It is a privilege to write a few words by way of Foreword to this Ruby year celebratory volume comprising a set of fine articles from the members of FFRRC Faculty edited by Fr. Dr Jose John. As a 'surviving' member of the founding Faculty in 1980 I rejoice in and marvel at the incredible way in which the three theological seminaries belonging to three different churches could collaborate in this truly ecumenical venture to offer higher theological education and research facilities to several generations of teachers and pastors in India. As a humble tribute to the great teachers and venerable leaders of our constituent seminaries and churches behind the Federated Faculty let me offer some modest reflections on the emerging context of our mission and ministry.

A fundamental feature of Christian discipleship is highlighted by Christ himself when in his final farewell prayer he asks God that his disciples may be granted grace to remain *in the world*, while being *not of the world* (Jn. 17:11-16). All forms of Christian mission and ministry arise from this twin vocation of being actively involved in the life of this world while constantly transcending and distancing from it. To lean unilaterally to one or the other side is to become either simply worldly with all its material preoccupations or be only other-worldly with all its negation of the world that God created out of love. In either case it would be the denial of the principle of incarnation of God in Christ Jesus. This is the challenge of the Gospel of Christ.

Human being is called a "border being" in the best of Patristic literature precisely because of this unique human calling to become a creative interface between the body and the soul, between the material and the spiritual. To the best of our knowledge no other species except the *homo sapiens* can assume this role. Our greatest mystery still is human consciousness that is conscious of itself and is able to transcend itself.

To be on the border is not an easy task. In Christian theological anthropology the border being has to be the medium of communication between the two realms. This implies a high degree of transparency and sensitivity on the part of humanity that is at the border. Human persons or humanity as a whole at the border cannot act like a thick wall that obstructs all communication. It would then be the wall of separation and division that Christ has demolished through his death according to Paul the Apostle. Instead the constant exchange and sharing between matter and spirit requires openness to both worlds.

Modern European thinking from the time of Descartes in the 17th century has been deeply marked by matter-spirit duality. The operational success of scientific methodology completely despised the spiritual realm. The rise of secularisation abolished all transcendent reference outside of the frame of spatiotemporal materiality. Main stream western secular-scientific thought thus thrived on Cartesian dichotomy of spirit and matter, and there was no way any exchange could be envisaged between them. There are even popular word-play jokes about this like, for example,: *"What is mind?"."Doesn't matter." "What is matter?"."Never mind"!*

This paradigm seems to have been shaken in the latter half of the 20th century when Quantum physics, life sciences, cognitive neurosciences, new cosmology, nanotechnology, global ecological awareness, bio-technologies, deep psychology, extrasensory perceptions, consciousness research and several interdisciplinary areas of exploring the mind-matter relationship have called into question the neat dualist and mechanistic world view. The innumerable dimensions of a multiverse or polyverse rather than a *uni*verse open up ever new configurations of Reality that defy definitions. For persons of some sensitivity this is simply mind-boggling and humbling. Traditional religious doctrinal paradigms of Reality are unable to cope with this.

In our contemporary digital age of Artificial Intelligence (AI), Quantum computing, Cyborgs, Internet of Things and various Human Enhancement bio-technologies, the mind-machine interface is swiftly getting thinner and thinner. Popular historian-prophet Yuval Noah Harari would say that 99% of all human professional capability will be easily taken over by AI. He would reduce everything to the all-pervasive algorithm, the step by step methodical procedure to do calculations or resolve problems. Although all organisms are regulated by congenital algorithms, there is no reason to think that non-organic algorithms will not take over all human activity from politics and economy to art and culture. Things considered impossible for machines a year ago are becoming efficiently operative part of our daily life. AI and Biotechnology will rule the world. Yet human consciousness still remains the deepest mystery, probably the last border for AI to cross over to outsmart or even totally erase us the Homo sapiens, our very human race, from the face of the earth. Artificial Intelligence has become the all-powerful competitor for Christian theological anthropological understanding of human nature and its divine potential.

Along with all these mind-shattering technological developments that challenge our conventional vision of the future shape of humanity, the heart-renting scream of millions of victims of war and violence, injustice, poverty and misery of all sorts never ceases to subvert all our dreams of a happy human race.

What then is the relevance of our theology, our ministry and mission in this context? The only model that gives us some certainty and hope is that of Christ. He addressed his followers as "the little sheepfold", and as the "salt of the earth", and "light of the world". These three images are symbols of humility, invisibility and weightlessness, and yet they are qualities that can transform our present world reality. These images suggest the qualities of the Church, the body of Christ, its mission and ministry in the world. We need to be reminded in all humility that the world scenario today might help us restore these prime qualities of the Church as Christ wanted it rather than indulge in some megalomaniacal and imperialistic dreams for the future.

■■■

Preface

The Federated Faculty for Research in Religion and Culture (FFRRC) is an academic institution committed to promote theological, philosophical, hermeneutical, and ecumenical discussions and deliberations. It tries to disseminate epistemological and methodological innovations within the academia and among the faith communities, irrespective of caste, creed, confessions and gender distinctions. FFRRC promotes a wider ecumenical vision rooted in the perichoretic understanding of the Holy Trinity revealed through the unfathomable love of Jesus Christ, the Word Incarnate.

The Federated Faculty for Research in Religion and Culture in Kerala is a pioneering ecumenical venture among the theological fraternity under the Senate of Serampore College. FFRRC was founded as a joint programme of the Orthodox Theological Seminary, Kottayam, the Mar Thoma Theological Seminary, Kottayam and the Kerala United Theological Seminary, Thiruvananthapuram, sponsored by the Orthodox Church, the Mar Thoma Church and the Dioceses of the Church of South India in Kerala.

It's a great privilege for me to greet you all on this auspicious occasion of the Ruby Jubilee Celebration of FFRRC. At this juncture I would like to recollect with great gratitude the pioneers and forerunners of FFRRC for their ecumenical Vision and Mission. I am for sure that everyone would agree with me that FFRRC could promote theological education in India with ecumenical spirit and collaboration for the last forty years. As a research centre, FFRRC has been promoting admirable theological education and research programmes in its academic mission. It has been a model for ecumenical fraternity and theological collaboration amidst theological and doctrinal diversities. It becomes a unique theological institution in India with great ecumenical spirit and cooperation.

Well, let me take this opportunity to introduce, with immense joy and pleasure, this book which commemorates the Ruby Jubilee Celebration of FFRRC. It's an effort to address the pandemic and post-pandemic situation with Faith and Trust in God. "*Towards a Relevant Ministry in the Post Pandemic Period*" in Biblical-theological and historical-ministerial perspectives is the theme of this book. There are more than thirteen articles which address the post-pandemic realities from biblical, theological, historical and ministerial perspectives. The book is entitled as, "**Witnessing Together: Forty Years of Ecumenical Theological Pilgrimage**". The FFRRC family is grateful to all those who are associated with the publication of this Jubilee commemorative volume. Fr. Dr. K.M. George, Director, Sopana Orthodox Academy and former principal of Orthodox Theological Seminary, Kottayam has graciously written the foreword note and blessed this academic exercise with his profound theological reflections. Our sincere thanks are due to all the contributors of this volume for their scholarly and challenging articles. On behalf of the FFRRC family, I would like to extend a word of gratitude to the Fr. Dr. Johns Abraham Konat (Chairperson till November 2021) and Fr. Dr. Reji Mathew (Chairperson since December 2021) for all their advices and scholarly inputs to make this volume a memorable one. The Co-chairpersons Rev. Dr. V.S. Varughese and Rev. Dr. C.I. David Joy and the treasurer Rev. Dr. L.V Bipinlal gave all necessary support for the successful completion of this project. The tireless and meticulous work of Rev. Dr. Koshy

P Varughese, the registrar of FFRRC, needs special appreciation. Without his support and earnest assistance this project would not have been materialized. The editorial board with Rev. Dr. C.I. David Joy, as convener, worked hard for this project. Special thanks to the executive committee members and all faculty colleagues and office staff for their constant support and encouragement. Special word of appreciation goes to Prof. Dr. Susan John for her meticulous and skillful contributions for the editing of this book. Rev. Dn. Jerin Johnson designed the cover page and our thanks are due to him. I am profoundly humbling myself that I could be part of this institution and its Ruby Jubilee Celebrations. I am sure that the publication of this book would be a great achievement and contribution of FFRRC to the ecumenical theological education in India.

Kottayam
15/03/22

Fr. Dr. Jose John
Editor

■■■

Becoming a Christian Community of Theological Imagination as Envisaged in the Epistle of Jude

Rev. Dr. C.I. David Joy

Introduction

The Ruby Jubilee of FFRRC is a clear statement of ecumenical witness and affirmation initiated by many visionaries, sustained in the grace of God and empowered by the Spirit of God. Therefore, I am delighted to state that this institution will continue to promote ecumenical witness in the field of theological education by training men and women to become teachers of theology.

The study of the Epistle of Jude, is important in the context of growing challenges and encounters in the church today. I clearly perceive that the ideas depicted in the Book of Jude could offer a proper password in terms of entering into the textual and theological world of early Christianity. [1] The theological world of early Christianity could be a symbolic world based on the social and political conditions of that time. It is best to study the location and identity of the false teachers in detail in order to identify the milieu of early Christianity. The presence of false teachers and opponents of the apostles had created a confusing atmosphere as far as the early church was concerned. It was most probably in the context of Palestinian Christianity that the Book of Jude emerged. Such a supposition is feasible because many ideas projected by the Palestine Christianity are visible and explicit in this book. A proper understanding of the Book of Jude is possible only by a proper study of various aspects of the book. One of those areas of study includes early Christology specifically Palestinian Christology in the first century.

It is not very clear whether Jude, the author of the book according to the textual evidence and James, the brother of our Lord Jesus could be the same person or two different persons. Any study of the Book of Jude becomes an important task today as it clearly reflects a higher level of Gnosticism than the one portrayed in the Pauline letters. The early Christian communities had encountered many issues associated with Gnosticism due to various concerns relating to the identity of the community. An ideology becoming the cornerstone of a community's identity is a distinctive feature in the New Testament World. Becoming a Christian community with the assistance of theological imagination had been part of Christian faith process in the first three centuries of the Christian era. This book, the Book of Jude, thus presents the identity of God encountered through Jesus Christ and uses the terminologies and theological framework of ecclesiology and eschatology.

In this book a theology of relationship can be seen between Jesus Christ and his followers by using the language for communication and life. Establishing the milieu of Jude thus becomes a prime task for studying the context of the Book of Jude. The milieu of the New Testament is a complex word and world as it is a mixture of the identity of the author, the world of the author, audience, implied reader and many more associated details. This letter has attracted me for three main reasons namely the unique language used by the author, the polemical nature of the contents of the book and the reflection of the community behind the book. According to the current trends in the study of the New Testament and the multidimensional tools used by its interpreters, it is noted that the process of the uncovering of the New Testament, specifically the Book of Jude in order to arrive at a proper meaning is not an easy task. Since it is part of the New Testament canon from the beginning of the canon of the New Testament, it is assumed that the reader of the New Testament considered this book a valuable and significant one in terms of protecting our faith. As has been mentioned earlier, the intent in studying this book is mainly to clearly address the issue of false teachers. Thus, this book provides a great many insights for identifying, analysing and addressing the issue of false teachings in the church today. During the pandemic, the "meaningless rhetoric" could not create an impact in the life and ministry of the Church. At the same time there have been many prayerful and systematic theological and ecclesial endeavours initiated by dedicated theological scholars and Churches to promote and nurture the faith of the Church.

It is important to note that Jude's approach in terms of raising many foundation-shaking encounters in the theological and ethical framework of the early church had brought unimaginable trouble to the author. Among the early Christian communities, many people, especially during the post-apostolic era, were confronted with the arguments raised by the opponents of Jude. It would be good to focus mainly on four things viz., a careful study of the Book of Jude in meticulous detail, the features of the gentile churches between 50 C.E-100 C.E, the theological form of Jude and significance of Jude in New Testament theology. It is not an easy task to explain the destination of the book as Jude deals with many concerns and issues encountered by the Gentile churches of the first stage of the post-Apostolic age. It must be noted that a clear dichotomy between the apostolic age and post apostolic age is not possible due to the complex and mixed content of this book. In the same way, a study on the basic features of gentile churches of the first century should be carried out in order to express the milieu of the book of Jude. A study of the Book of Jude is very important in today's church. A study of all the gentile churches in the first century C.E is not possible; therefore an attempt is made to identify the churches closer to the heart of the Book of Jude. As far as the theological ideas of Jude are concerned, it is significant to note that Jude had intended to address issues related to the identity and existence of the early Christian communities. Indeed, a close study of the Book of Jude will certainly shed more light in terms of understanding the significance of the New Testament theology today.

It is suggested to apply sociological methods to study the Book of Jude in order to understand the social world of the Book of Jude in a legitimate manner. It is assumed that the readers may approach the book with some basic New Testament knowledge, so that they can understand the social world of early Christianity very well. Since the author uses some images and metaphors from nature, ethnographic studies might offer some additional help in understanding the Book of Jude. New Testament ethnography is a new branch of sociological studies and is still at the beginning stage of research. However, wherever it is applied sensibly a good result could be produced for understanding the world of the New Testament and different layers of meaning of the New Testament.

The Early Church-An Overview

One of the very fascinating areas of the studies of the New Testament is the question of social institutions in the early church. It is not an easy task to identify, define and derive the basic features of the early church due to its multi-axial identity. While glorifying the sociological method which seems to be the culmination of the historical-cultural method of the New Testament and recognising its fruitfulness in bringing out the meaning of the sociological units in the early church, it is noted that substantial studies had been done by scholars like J. Bingham (1850), Adolf Deissmann (1908) and Albert Schweitzer about the basics of the early church. Among their works Joseph Bingham's *Origins Ecclesiastics: The Antiquity of the Christian Church*, is a very scholarly and well-designed book which influenced the research activities of many generations.[2] It is significant because Joseph Bingham used Philo and many other dependable authors of the first century who analytically and critically wrote about the nature of the early church. It is noted that Philo used the term "Jesseans: either from Jesse the father of David or which is more probable, from the name of the Lord Jesus".[3] Bingham's study is very helpful in understanding the basics of the early church as he categorized early Christianity from the various points of view regarding their identities in connection with the reception of Jude. Thomas R. Schreiner argued that the letter was authentic and of first century origin.[4] Then a study about the first century Gentile church seems to be very appropriate and fitting. Since Jude used Jewish traditions in his epistle, it is possible to consider that the recipients of the letter included some Jewish Christians too. Many destinations proposed include Alexandria, Palestine, Syria, Asia Minor and Egypt. There are a number of studies pointing to this aspect, citing the Alexandrian origin of the Book of Jude.

I continue to explore the features of the first century churches so that there may be some foundation for a meaningful exposition of the Book of Jude. It is important to identify and analyse every theological and ideological institution found in the Book of Jude for a correct understanding of the content and significance of the book. There is no doubt at all that the Book of Jude played a key role in addressing the issue of Gnosticism in the first century Gentile and Jewish churches. In the writings of Philo, the early followers of Jesus had been the elect ones who became the channels of transformation. Such an understanding about the early Christians by Philo indicated the real life situation and significance of the early followers of Jesus.[5] As has been mentioned earlier, Joseph Bingham's study will certainly help researchers to understand the milieu of Jude in a better and more systematic manner than the present research conclusion about the milieu of the Book of Jude.

The places like Alexandria or Egypt could be a possibility due to the ideology of the opponents in the Book of Jude. This paper attempts to locate a closer milieu and destination in order to locate the significance and meaning of the identity of the author of the Book of Jude.

While talking about the early church, there are stereotyped research conclusions available today. However, Joseph Bingham's work is different from that of many of his contemporary scholars. The first century church whom Jude addresses might be a church that encountered several spiritual and parenetical questions and concerns posed by the heretics in the early church. Therefore, only through a systematic study of the early church can one arrive at a clear conclusion about the authorship and destination of Jude.

In the early church it was an acceptable fact that early eye witness accounts of the Jesus movement had been considered to be the most dependable for reconstituting the socio-cultural and religious dimensions of the church. The socio cultural and religious dimensions of the early church should be studied in order to analyse various features of the early church which will in turn guide the readers to further explore the foundations of the early church.

Regarding the first century gentile church, the most remarkable feature is its communitarian nature. Headed by the apostolic ethics and leadership, there is ample resonance in the Book of Jude in terms of early Christian Gentile nature and textual world. The most significant difference between first century Jewish Christian church and first century Gentile Christian church was the difference in identity. Only be applying an appropriate sociological theory can this difference be exhibited well. This argument is clearly endorsed by Francois Bovon in his 2003 book *Studies in Early Christianity* by exploring various themes in the New Testament.[6] For Bovon, it is important to consider the arguments and expositions that emerge within the framework and milieu of early Christian communities. Such arguments and expositions will initiate a new avenue for entering into the world of early Christianity, especially the non-Jewish Christianity. There is no intention here to cause a dichotomy between Jewish Christianity and Non-Jewish Christianity as there were many similarities between those communities in terms of their theology, faith, doctrine and liturgy. However, a major difference that could be noticed here is the difference in their cultural and linguistic identity. It is noted that cultural dynamics of the gentile Christianity makes it absolutely necessary to learn more about the Book of Jude. Francois Bovon clearly states that, "it seems as if the entire Christian construction is based not on Christ alone, but on the fulfilment of the Holy Scriptures through Jesus Christ as preached and accepted by the apostolic church.[7]

How did the scholars evaluate the formation of Christianity, specifically in the matter of the early Christianity? It is believed that Jude was written to a group of Christians in the post-Apostolic era and the Book of Jude indeed dealt with the question of identity of the early Christians. The identity question was not addressed from the point of view of scripture alone but from the multi-layered approach which will pinpoint the real world of early Christianity. As a researcher in the field of the New Testament it is seen that there had been a conflict in the early Christianity on preserving the apostolic memory. New Testament scholars consider the oral tradition for preserving the memory of the church. When it comes in terms of apostolic memory it is noted that there were many explicit and implicit institutions and organizations in transmitting the memory in its true sense and the Book of Jude was one among then. Francois Bovon further states:

> Further Confirmation of this relevance of memory can be found in three related phenomena that occurred within early Christian tradition building: First, in the intellectual dimension that the apostles were not numerous individuals but members of a constituted group, a board of religious leaders: Second, in the slow merging of two originally distinct categories, the twelve called by the historical Jesus and the apostles sent by the resurrected Lord: and third, in the additional dimension of locating Paul in either category.[8]

What is unique in Jude in terms of comprehending this claim? It is observed that a study of the Book of Jude can indeed inspire and offer new directions in studying the features and identity of the early Christianity in a very systematic way. It is systematic on two grounds: doctrinal clarity and ecclesial dimensions. My intention and intent to locate the Book of Jude is the basis of such enquiry. The religious and cultural strength of the Book of Jude has been evident in the context and the use of the book by the churches in the region of Asia Minor. The geographical context of the Book of Jude is only an assumption as many scholars consider even the authorship with pseudonymity. Since the name Jude was associated with the family of Jesus, it was clearly acceptable to the early church.

The socio-cultural context of early Christianity both Jewish and gentile, has been studied, analysed and constituted by many scholars by taking the characters and events revealed in the New Testament into account. However, many views have been expressed with clarity by proposing the theological and ecclesial scenes clearly. Since the chapter deals with the context of early church for placing the Book of Jude within the framework of early Christianity it is important to locate the context because of the message of the Book of Jude and its literary dependence. The respect for the Book of Jude in the early Church and the impact the message could make within the cultural and theological context of the church will be counted. I am interested in explaining the study further mainly because of the multi-faceted impact of Book of Jude and its message.

Political Horizons

Another significant dimension in the context of the early church is the political implications of the early church. When I say political, I should start with the Roman imperial power institutions that encountered and challenged the basic features of early Christianity.

In the recent past, there have been outstanding and ground breaking explanations contributed by many New Testament scholars who indeed offer new directions and avenues for research. To mention a few one should bring forth the contributions of Richard Horsley, Helmut Koester, Sean Freyne and Gerd Theissen. Since it is dealt with the context mainly for studying the Book of Jude, I will only mention basic features and significant contributions for discussion.

In one of the recent studies conducted by Joseph Plevik, *Paul and Parousia*, he argues that the context of the New Testament should be explained by taking the history of the apocalyptic and eschatological community seriously as both dimensions could design and determine the basic agenda for a meaningful interpretation of the book of Jude.[9] Therefore, it is considered that the explanations done by Gerd Theissen in terms of the interdisciplinary and multidisciplinary social system of culture should be considered a foundational starting point of the study of the first century early church specifically addressed by Jude.

The first century Roman Empire and the neo-colonial forces now should be evaluated by asking the question of how the situation of the ordinary people is different from that of the socially higher ranked people. Jude, as mentioned earlier, presented the agonies and aspiration of the people of God, specifically the followers of Jesus Christ, despite the empire mobilisation in terms of exploitation and oppression. The challenge of a postcolonial cultural exegesis in Jude lies in the ability of the early Christian communities in addressing the conflicts and encounters in the first century Roman Empire.

Claims are put forward regarding Jude as a servant of Jesus Christ who was sanctified by his experiences in the Lord. This sanctification is a process of preservation in the Lord in terms of addressing the challenges posed by the Roman Empire. In the power status of the Roman Empire there is a disproportionate exclusion of the common people. The first century church is revealed in Jude in many ways. The relationship between the social system and the emerging ecclesial models in the first century is a true subject for study.

The predominant sentiment in the first century ecclesiology was the acceptance of Christ as the centre of the universe. This act of dedication and understanding was in tune with their total dependence on the Lord. The disciples of Jesus began to teach the people of God the need for a community of mutual acceptance and forgiveness. In order to locate the context of Jude and his message it is important to revisit the first century church from various viewpoints. In the recent past, New Testament scholars developed methodological tools and frameworks to address the issue of the identity of the early church with the help of social sciences and research tools. Since the methodological tools helped the readers of the New Testament, they could arrive at convincing conclusions about the status and identity of the early church. The study of Jude is significant as this claim is very much evident in the text.

The development of Christian communities in new regions had been a major event in the context of imperial power structures. It is not an easy task to recover the structure and framework of the formation of the early church in the first century due to the methodological and epistemological considerations. E. Ferguson's 1996 book *The Church of Christ: A Biblical Ecclesiology* is one of the ground breaking research tools to understand the identity of the early church.[10] Jude presents some aspects of the ecclesiology and challenges associated with the functioning of the church in the early period. The issues of harmony and conflicts between the early Christian communities indeed created a lot of problems in the first century. However, the miracle was the clear framework of early Christian doctrines and declaration of the basic faith by the early Christian communities. In Jude there are multiple layers of social and cultural expression in addressing the issues associated with ecclesiology. The Roman Empire imposed taxes on every commodity as part of their economic policies. The administrative element thus became very oppressive in nature. At every stage of the Hellenistic empires there were mainly two types of taxes namely direct tax and indirect tax. The tax system divided the people in the light of their citizenship and civil rights.[11] It is important to understand the basics of Greek religion and culture in order to study about the formation of the early church as the Greek religion and culture paved the way for the formation of the Roman religious and imperial framework. All kinds of indirect taxes were levied on the non-citizens of the land. It was not very easy for a person, an outsider, to be given the status of citizenship in the Roman Empire. The citizenship had been associated with a number of privileges and responsibilities. Most of the taxes imposed on the citizens were duties, sales taxes, market taxes and part taxes. In addition to those there were many other taxes which could create an atmosphere of oppression and exploitation in the society. The more the Roman Empire occupied new regions and kingdoms the more they imposed taxes such as head taxes, property taxes and commercial licence fee for adding income to the imperial government to meet the expenses of the army and navy.[12] As a result the poor and the marginalized became the victims of the tax system. The early church could attract marginalised people with its ideology of accommodating the ignored and the oppressed people with the values of the gospel.

By applying the scale of sociological tools, modern readers of religions have tried to understand the growth of the early church in many ways. The major conclusion arrived at was that the early church could brilliantly exploit the situation of conflict between the Roman citizens and the non-citizens. Therefore, the non-citizens moved their dependence and loyalty to the new religion namely Christianity. It is also noted that the Christian religion offered a new sense of identity and status to the people who looked for a space and location to move forward. It was the custom of the Greek empire to formulate a society in the light of the cultural speciality of Hellenism and cultural elements related to it. As a result, an elite group had emerged as a constituency of scholars, physician, merchants and so on. They became the beneficiaries of imperial power and naturally their loyalty was purely with the imperial administration. Eventually, thousands of public servants and military personnel constituted a support group and were part of the imperial policies. As a result, the people of the margins could not get into the framework of the imperial power. The picture of the early church specifically depicted in Jude is that of a body that could successfully offer space for the other. It is indeed a tantalizing piece of information about the identity of the early Christians. According to Jude the post Apostolic period is a period of encounters and confrontations in terms of false teachers in the church. Therefore, it is very vital to know about the socio-cultural context of the origin and development of the early church.

The early church emerged in the context of the Roman republic which was controlled by the imperial policies. The overarching political domination was designed by the Senate which consisted of the leaders of the patrician families. Due to the clashes among the patricians another group emerged, and the result was instability in the empire. A series of civil wars and communal clashes determined the destiny of the people of the land. The Senate was not interested in solving these problems, but in protecting its vested interests, particularly economic interests. The Caesars namely Pompey and Gaius Julius made a lot of oppressive policies in the first century B.C.E. At the time of Jesus' birth Augustus was the Caesar, the emperor. His original name was Octavian. However, in 27 B.C.E he was conferred the title, Augustus. The title Augustus means the carrier of divine law. By exercising his power in a brutal manner, he controlled Egypt, Syria, Gaul and Spain. Though the empire had undergone a period of civil war and crisis during his period, he secured absolute domination over the provinces. His descendants originated from his daughter Julia as he had no son.[13] Tiberius was the emperor from 14 CE to 37 CE while Jesus was doing his ministry during his period. The early church emerged clearly during the times of Caligula, Claudius, Nero and Titus Flavius Vespasianus and Domitian. It was Domitian who demanded the people of the empire to address him as "Lord and God".[14] That scenario created a kind of severe persecution of Christians. The Book of Jude is analysed by taking all those political aspects into account.

{Rev. Dr. C.I. David Joy, an ordained priest of the Church of South India, is the principal of Kerala United Theological Seminary and the co-chairperson of the FFRRC. He is a member of SBL-IVBS and a board member of SBL-ICI. He is specialised in the branch of New Testament and authored many books and articles.}

Endnotes

[1] C.I. David Joy, Jude: Window to the Early Church, Bangalore : Omega Books, 2021.

[2] Joseph Bingham, *Origins Ecclesiastics: The Antiquity of the Christian Church*, 1850

[3] Ibid., p.7

[4] Thomas R. Schreiner, Jude: The New American Commentary, Louisville: Broadman & Hodman Publication, 2003, p.409.

[5] Joseph, Bingham, op.cit., p.1.

[6] Francois Bovon, *Studies in Early Christianity*, 2003

[7] Ibid. p.5.

[8] Ibid p.7.

[9] Joseph Plevnik, Paul and Parousia, Eugene: WIPE 1997.

[10] Ferguson, The Church of Christ: A Biblical Ecclesiology for Today, Grand Rapids MI; Eerdmans, 1996.

[11] Hetmut Koester, History, Culture and Religion of the Hellenistic Age, Vol. 1. De Grutyer, 1995.

[12] Ibid., p.283.

[13] Ibid., p.30.

[14] Ibid., p.30.

■■■

Multidimensionality of Ministry from a Prophetic Perspective

Rev. Dr. M.C. Thomas

Introduction

The distinctiveness of the prophetic ministry of ancient Israel was widely found in the alternative and radical nature which was exhibited in its discourses and practices. As a matter of fact, it addressed the community with alternative imaginations which has explicitly been explained by Walter Brueggemann in his book The *Prophetic Imagination* (2001). He writes

> The task of prophetic ministry is to nurture, nourish, and evoke a consciousness and perception alternative to the consciousness and perception of the dominant culture around us... The alternative consciousness to be nurtured serves to *criticize* in dismantling the dominant consciousness. Also, on the other hand, it serves to *energize* persons and communities by its promise of another time and situation toward which the community of faith may move.[1]

Grounded on these fundamental principles of prophetic ministry, this paper will briefly attempt to unravel the energizing element of the prophetic ministry of Elijah and Elisha as described in the Book of Kings.

Multidimensional Ministry of the Prophets Elijah and Elisha

The prophetic stories of Elijah and Elisha do not offer precise historical accounts, but they feature amazing and even fantastic descriptions about the multidimensionality of their ministry in the Northern Kingdom of Israel during the 9th century BCE. Moreover, unlike the biblical accounts on the Omride dynasty with their strict Yahwistic and Deuteronomistic bias and coloring, these stories about the prophets appear less propagandistic but more legendary in presenting the prophets as holy men of God with the power to mediate with prophetic imagination. Furthermore, the prophets Elijah and Elisha had been venerated as local heroes by the people who had largely been empowered by their diversified ministry.

These stories give prominence to the common people and their cultural experiences. As Judith A. Todd states, the Elijah-Elisha cycle features "stories that give voice to the traditional values that were under pressure from the socio-economic policies of the state."[2]Generally these stories "focus on the practical concern of a marginal community for food, shelter, tools and healing,"[3]which doesn't mean that the activity of the prophets was confined only to the lower strata of the society. Elisha had constant contact with the people of high rank as well. For instance, the "great lady" of Shunem was a person of high status, and further in 2 Kings 4:42 we learn of an anonymous person from Baal-Shalishah who brought food and gifts to Elisha and he (Elisha or the man from Baal-Shalishah) said, "give (them) to the people." In short, as Tanis Hoover Rentería has pointed out, these stories project a social world "outside the monarchic circle and in fundamental conflict with it."[4]Moreover, besides the main characters, that is, the prophets Elijah and Elisha, Ziony Zevit points to the other characters as "types" or "a cross-section of the common folk," viz., a widow, a prophetic band of *ben' y neb§ § m* (sons of the prophets), a certain man, etc.[5] As Alexander Rofé has observed, "Nothing is told of their origins, histories, physical appearances, opinions, thoughts, desires or deeds. Not even their names are provided… Likewise, nothing is told about their character, thoughts, feelings, deeds, family relations, social and economic rank."[6]

Also, as indicated, with regard to the beneficiaries of the prophetic ministry, it seems that the followers of Elijah and Elisha were heterogeneous in their religious beliefs, practices and socio-economic status. As Scott D. Hill suggests, there does not seem to be "uniformity among the followers of Elijah or Elisha on any issue or conflict, whether Yahwistic, anti-Omride, or in favour of any particular class."[7] What unifies them, is the prophet who as Hill notes, is the local hero, the man of God, Elijah and/or Elisha. Hill defines local heroes as men or women who are "recognized as 'holy' in conjunction with the shifting balances in social forces."[8] The holiness refers to their "privileged access to power," their ability to perform miracles, or their capacity to "overturn a power group."[9] For many, at least, of the common people, "allegiance to monotheistic faith has been less important than their loyalty to the local hero."[10] Each village may have had its own local hero or heroes. Hill says, "They may influence the conception, birth, and health of children; the success of crops, business ventures, marriages and partnerships; safety in travel and work, natural phenomena such as rainfall, plagues and wild animals."[11] The role and function of Elijah and Elisha as represented by most of the Elijah-Elisha cycle support this observation.

Furthermore, as men of empowerment, Elijah and Elisha project the identity of the common people during ninth century Israel. In that sense, being a minority, they-particularly Elijah (but not so clearly Elisha)-were outside the centre and served as spokespersons against the establishment.[12] Lawrence J. Taylor, in his article "Stories of Power, Powerful Stories: The Drunken Priest in Donegal," attempts to reveal the dynamic nature of the relationship between different religious groups through the stories of drunken priests. These powerful stories are never set in an official ecclesiastical context and are local compositions. He says, "They can be understood…as a people's creative response to their experience of religious power."[13] The local drunken priest walks within the realm of the common people and acts against the "ever-extending hegemony of the institutional church."[14] He is the "silenced" priest from the viewpoint of official religion because he is "anomalous" and "liminal" to them, yet he functions as the people's voice.[15] These are the stories of empowerment by ordinary popular religious groups. The stories themselves and their mode of communication function as counter-hegemonic to the establishment. Towards the end of the famine, for example, when Ahab met Elijah, Ahab asked him, "Is that you, you troubler of Israel?" (1 Kgs 18: 16-17). Elijah, being a "troubler," was "liminal" and "anomalous"in the perspective of Ahab and the Omrides who represent the establishment. From Elijah's perspective, however, it is the misguided king who is the "troubler" of Israel (1 Kgs 18:18).

Why are these miracle stories included in the larger Deuteronomistic history? Perhaps, sociologically, these stories reveal the distressful socio-economic condition of the people under the Omrides and perhaps under Jehu as well, and point to the prophetic empowerment of these people.[16]According to Rentería, "What is most important in these stories is not the empirical nature of the prophetic powers, but the interactions between the prophet who offers his mediating skills and the people in need of a better connection with the power that provides health, food, and reproduction."[17] The prophet, as a man of God, has such divine power. The commoners approach the prophet for the remedy and solution of their problems, cure of their sickness or barrenness, resuscitation of the dead, etc.

Ministry within the Prophetic Bands

The prophetic ministry appears to be performed within multiple social settings. Some of the miracles recorded in the Elijah-Elisha cycle were carried out within the prophetic bands. Reference to the prophetic bands appears predominantly in the Elisha stories and we have only limited information regarding their nature, group-structure and social function within the Northern Kingdom. As Cogan and Tadmor suggest, they "appear as loosely organized brotherhoods living together in the towns of northern Israel and are referred to mostly in the Elisha story cycle. They are not associated with local shrines, as is sometimes claimed, and are probably to be distinguished from the prophets consulted by the Omride kings (e.g., 1 Kgs 22:6)."[18] Moreover, no precise chronological indication regarding these "miraculous" actions is evident in the stories. Most of the stories reflect the context of natural calamities like drought and famine and the resultant poverty among the people which was a common feature in an agrarian community. The socio-historical settings, as Cogan and Tadmor indicate, appear "secondary in importance to these stories which heap praise upon the prophetic master."[19]

Regarding the death of Elijah (2 Kgs 2:1-12), it is recorded that he "ascended to heaven in a storm" (vv. 1, 11), which, of course, has a miraculous character, and was witnessed by only a small group of the prophetic bands. According to Cogan and Tadmor, "By utilizing this image, the prophet's followers invested him with the quality of eternal life, surpassing even Moses, the father of all prophets, who died and was buried (albeit by God himself: Deut

34:5-6). It was this quality which became the dominant motif in the later Elijah legends."[20]

Moreover, Elisha and (probably the prophetic bands) also addressed Elijah, as Elijah was ascending to heaven in a whirlwind, by "Oh, my father, my father! The chariots of Israel and its horsemen!" (2 Kgs 2:12). The prophetic succession of Elisha, as Cogan and Tadmor observe, "to the 'fathership' over the Sons of the Prophets is demonstrated by his ability to perform the wondrous splitting of the Jordan; he has indeed inherited his master's qualities. The mantle of Elijah which he now wears is apparently the same one thrown over him when he first met Elijah (see 1 Kgs 19:19-21), though such identity is not made explicit."[21] In addition, 2 Kgs 6:1-7 records the miracle of Elisha in helping the man (presumably one of the prophetic band) to retrieve his borrowed axe-head that had fallen into the river. As the loss of the borrowed axe would make his economic condition significantly worse its recovery is very important. Elisha's miracle of purifying the stew and making it edible (2 Kgs 4:38-41) shows

> "Just another type of interaction between prophet and follower in which powerless individuals take action to change their situation. The story shows that Elisha not only feeds his followers, but also enables them to overcome the daily hazards of trying to eat during a famine."[22] For the waters that had proven to be bad and harmful, "Elisha, as YHWH's messenger, effects a cure which makes them potable, thus restoring life to the townspeople. Tales such as this, of miraculous, sustaining acts by holy men of God, are part of the traditional lore–legenda–of prophetic circles."[23]

Moreover, 2 Kgs 4:1-7 narrates the life situation of the prophetic bands. The widow, after the death of her husband, faced loss of her children to debt slavery. The woman refers to her husband as 'your servant' (v.1), which indicates "the relationship between Elisha and the sons of the prophets."[24] According to Wesley J. Bergen, "As rhetoric, the term also places Elisha in a position of obligation, as one responsible for the well-being of this individual."[25] Bergen adds that, "Elisha, as man of God (v.7), is further placed in a position of obligation both by the late husband's fear of YHWH and by his knowledge of this fact."[26] Moreover, for Bergen, in their distressful, unprotected and helpless social condition, it "is only the intercession of the great man of God that allows for salvation from economic and familial ruin. This world cannot survive without the miraculous, and even the miraculous can only save by providing a surplus of saleable goods."[27] In summary, what we have noticed is that the prophetic miracle stories have a social setting within the prophetic bands where the community related to these holy men. It witnessed them as men of power and in return the community was empowered by their miracles.

Ministry Beyond Geographical Borders

The mission and "miraculous" actions of Elijah and Elisha were said to be performed within a larger community as well, even outside the borders of the Northern Kingdom. The provision of food in the wilderness for Elijah through the ravens suggests the empowerment of the prophet by Yahweh through miraculous ways. For Cogan, "The location and the means by which YHWH sustained Elijah, in a desert wadi and by ravens, accent the miraculous aspect of his gracious care of his servant."[28] The location of the Wadi Cherith is "unidentified," which is less significant from the perspective of the narrator.[29] In Zarephath, outside the borders of Israel, "Elijah proved YHWH's omnipotence; he was not limited to one land, because it was he who had brought the drought upon Israel just as he had upon Tyre; it was he who provided food to those who believed in him..."[30]

The story in 2 Kgs 4:42-44 describes the feeding of the crowd by Elisha. According to Rentería, this crowd reveals that "...Elisha attracted large groups of people. We have no way of knowing just what they were coming to Elisha for–perhaps teaching, healing, food, or as members of some clan trying to gain his patronage. He also has well-to-do supporters who send him provisions, something already evidenced by his relationship to the Shunammite in the earlier story."[31] In short, the prophetic activities were not confined within the inner circles of prophetic band, but the miracles and mission of empowerment extended to others beyond the borders of the North.

Ministry among the Marginalized Groups: Women and the Poor

As mentioned above, the Elijah-Elisha stories particularly reflect the experience of women and peasants who had become powerless and marginalized under the Omrides. They appear here as popular religious groups, economically backward and marginalized. On the other hand, these marginalized groups are represented as support group of the prophets through mutual empowerment. Rentería sees the relationship between the man of God and these support groups as "transactional"; for example, in the case of the widow of Zarephath, "he will empower her, and she will feed him."[32] The narrator of the story was addressing "people who, like this widow, had been victimized by the harsh conditions of famine and the structural inequalities of the monarchic system. People like this probably felt powerless to change the desperate conditions under which they lived. The prophet's power provided an alternative to despair."[33] In 1 Kgs 17, Elijah is sent by God to Zarephath of Sidon where a poor widow feeds him. In return the widow is empowered with meal and oil through a miraculous action by the prophet Elijah. It is interesting to note that the three characters in this story – the woman as widow, her son as fatherless and Elijah as sojourner – symbolize the three marginal groups who received the special concern and protection of Yahweh in the legal codes and elsewhere. Later in the story we see further empowerment of the widow by Elijah's resuscitation of her son (1 Kgs 17:17-24). Similarly, Elisha increases the oil for a widow, the wife of one of the deceased prophets in the prophetic band, and thereby prevents her sons being enslaved on account of debt (2 Kgs 4:1ff).[34] With regard to barrenness, a curse to women of any status within Israel, Elisha blessed the rich Shunamite woman with progeny and she gave birth to a son (2 Kgs 4:17).[35] She is described as "the great lady", which means, as Bergen observes, "wealthy, powerful, forthright."[36]According to Montgomery and Gehman, this story also shows "the woman's true intuition of bringing the prophet himself to her house, not accepting his servant as intermediary."[37] Also, she initially refused the offer of any help the prophet extended in return for her hospitality. Her reply that "I dwell among my own people," (v.13) indicates her social well-being, though she was barren. She did not, however, decline the promise of a son. Moreover, later in the story, when the son died, the Shunamite woman approaches the man of God, Elisha, seeking his favour, a practice which, as we indicated before, reflects popular religion in the Levant. Consequently Elisha (with God's help, though that is not emphasized) resuscitates her son from death (2 Kgs 4: 18-37).

The peasants in general - not only some women of the peasant class - were a group victimized by the uprooting of the traditional culture and values by the Omrides but favored by Elijah and Elisha. According to Rentería, "Peasants are rural cultivators who are persuaded or coerced to give up much of their produce, money and labour to a dominant class. Members of the dominant class use these "surpluses" to support their own standard of living and to support other groups in the society, such as artisans, retainers and priests, who do not farm but require payment for their goods and services."[38]Moreover, some of the miracles in these cycles are closely interconnected with the peasant community. As noted above, the oil and corn motifs in these miracles are related to a peasant economy. The rain motif in the miracles is also dealing with something very determinative for the peasant community. Famine and drought threatened the community during this period, especially those without surplus resources, and the supply of rainfall controls agriculture and thereby the production of grain and oil. 2 Kgs 7:1-3 shows that Elisha predicts an abundance of food after a severe famine in the land. Importantly, the Elijah-Elisha cycle narrates the experience of the marginal groups - along with or as a part of the popular religious groups - in the North particularly the women and the peasants and their multiple interactions with the holy men of God. Basically, these stories express how the men of God have responded to and related to the basic human needs and how the marginalized have experienced the intervention of God through these holy men of God.

Conclusion

The stories on the prophets Elijah and Elisha are in the nature of a dramatic elaboration of the miraculous deeds of these holy men of God, venerating them as local heroes. Since the biblical accounts of these prophets represent Deuteronomistic/pro-Judaean perspectives, and put forward considerable legendary elements in emphasizing the miraculous powers of the men of God like Elijah and Elisha, we face extensive difficulty in determining the real picture of the religious practices in the Northern Kingdom under the Omrides. But the stories in the Elijah-Elisha cycle present Elijah and Elisha as the local heroes, the men of God, endowed with divine power who had performed their ministry with strong prophetic imagination. Their engagements with the common populace, especially women, the fatherless and the marginalized, present these holy men as providing guidance and remedies for the people's problems, healing the sick and even raising the dead which prove the multi-dimensionality of their ministry in ancient Israel. These stories are concerned with the day-to-day life and existential concerns of the common populace as they face natural calamities, sickness, poverty, death and the like.

{Rev. Dr. M.C. Thomas is an ordained priest of the Mar Thoma Syrian Church, serving as a Professor and Research Guide in the department of Old Testament at the Mar Thoma Theological Seminary and the Federated Faculty for Research in Religion and Culture, (FFRRC) Kottayam. He has published many articles and books.}

Endnotes

[1] Walter Brueggemann, *The Prophetic Imagination* (0, 13.

[2] Judith A. Todd, "The Pre-Deuteronomistic Elijah Cycle," in, *Elijah and Elisha in Socioliterary Perspective* (Edited by Robert B. Coote; Atlanta: Scholars Press, 1992), 1.

[3] Todd, "The Pre-Deuteronomistic Elijah Cycle," 8.

[4] Renteria, Tanis Hoover. "The Elijah/Elisha Stories: A Socio-cultural Analysis of Prophets and People in Ninth-Century BCE Israel." In *Elijah and Elisha in Socioliterary Perspective*. (Edited by Robert B. Coote; Atlanta: Scholars Press, 1992), 76.

[5] Zevit, Ziony, The Religions of Ancient Israel: A Synthesis of Parallactic Approaches. (Continuum: London & New York, 2001), 489.

[6] Rofe, Alexander. "The Classification of the Prophetical Stories." *Journal of Biblical Literature* 89 (1970), 431.

[7] Scott D. Hill, "The Local Hero in Palestine in Comparative Perspective," in, *Elijah and Elisha in Socioliterary Perspective* (Edited by Robert B. Coote; Atlanta: Scholars Press, 1992), 38.

[8] Hill, "The Local Hero in Palestine," 39.

[9] Hill, "The Local Hero in Palestine," 39.

[10] Hill, "The Local Hero in Palestine," 39.

[11] Hill, "The Local Hero in Palestine," 42.

[12] Wilson identifies them as the "peripheral" prophets who operated outside the establishment. See, Robert R. Wilson, *Prophecy and Society in Ancient Israel* (Philadelphia: fortress Press, 1980), 195.

[13] Lawrence J. Taylor, "Stories of Power, Powerful Stories: The Drunken Priest in Donegal," in *Religious Orthodoxy & Popular Faith in European Society*, (edited by Ellen Badone; Princeton: Princeton University Press, 1990), 166.

[14] Taylor, "Stories of Power, Powerful Stories," 166.

[15] Taylor, "Stories of Power, Powerful Stories," 178.

[16] See, Rentería, "The Elijah/Elisha Stories," 77.

[17] Rentería, "The Elijah/Elisha Stories," 97.

[18] Cogan Mordecai and HayimTadmor, *II Kings: A New Translation with Introduction and Commentary*, vol. 11, Anchor Bible, edited by W.F. Albright and D.N. Freedman, (New York: Doubleday & company, 1988), 31.

[19] Cogan and Tadmor, *II Kings*, 59.

[20] Cogan and Tadmor, *II Kings*, 33-34.

[21] Cogan and Tadmor, *II Kings*, 34.

[22] Rentería, "The Elijah/Elisha Stories," 110-111.

[23] Cogan and Tadmor, *II Kings*, 37, citing comparison with "'eulogies' of saints and pious rabbis."

[24] Wesley J. Bergen, *Elisha and the End of Prophetism* (JSOTSS 286, Sheffield: Sheffield Academic Press, 1999), 84.

[25] Bergen, *Elisha and the End of Prophetism*, 84.

[26] Bergen, *Elisha and the End of Prophetism*, 84.

[27] Bergen, *Elisha and the End of Prophetism*, 86-87.

[28] Mordechai Cogan, *1 Kings, A New Translation with Introduction and Commentary*, vol. 10, Anchor Bible, edited by W.F. Albright and D.N. Freedman, (New York: Doubleday & company, 2001), 432.

[29] Cogan, *1 Kings*, 426.

[30] Cogan, *1 Kings*, 432.

[31] Rentería, "The Elijah/Elisha Stories," 112.

[32] See, Rentería, "The Elijah/Elisha Stories," 102.

[33] Rentería, "The Elijah/Elisha Stories," 102.

[34] Cf. Leah Bronner, *The Stories of Elijah and Elisha as Polemics Against Baal Worship* (Leiden: E.J. Brill, 1968), 83.

[35] According to Rentería, "Her interests as a woman in such a patriarchal society are protected only when she provides a son for the family. A woman without a son, no matter how wealthy, holds only a tentative place in the family of her husband. In such a patrilineal, patrilocal system, a woman leaves her own family to live with her husband's family, and her children belong to her husband's lineage. As an outsider to this household, she has little power or status until she bears children and has grown sons to protect her interests." Rentería, "The Elijah/Elisha Stories," 105.

[36] Bergen, *Elisha and the End of Prophetism*, 87.

[37] Montgomery and Gehman, *the Books of Kings*, 367.

[38] Rentería, "The Elijah/Elisha Stories," 93; cf. Eric R. Wolf, *Peasants* (Englewood Cliffs, New Jersey: Prentice Hall, Inc., 1966), 1-4, 9.

■■■

Theological Education in the 21St Century: Some Reflections

Rev. Dr. Abraham Philip

I am indeed very happy to contribute an article to the Ruby volume of FFRRC and I thank the Registrar Rev. Dr Koshy P Varghese for this opportunity. The FFRRC is completing 40 years of its existence. The last four decades almost mark my period of active ordained ministry in the Church. During that time, for more than two decades I have been part and parcel of FFRRC. My association with FFRRC began in the early 90s . The Rev. Dr. M J Joseph, the founding Registrar of FFRRC advised me to validate my M. Phil. degree from Wycliffe Hall, Oxford, England with the Senate of Serampore College. When I made the application, the Senate advised me to write a couple examinations at the M. Th level to qualify for it. Hence, I attended some seminars/ classes at the FFRRC while I was serving as the Director of Dr Thomas Mar Athanasius Memorial Orientation Centre, Manganam. The seminars/classes were led/taken by the Rev. Dr. M. V. Abraham, the then Principal of MTTS and Rev. Dr. Cherian Thomas, the then Registrar of FFRRC. The present Registrar, Rev Dr Koshy P Varghese was also one of the students of that class. After the validation of my degree, I was permitted to do doctoral research in the field of New Testament. At that time, I was Vicar of Karol Bagh Marthoma parish, New Delhi. The Senate of Serampore had only one doctoral centre at that time and it was SATHRI, Bangalore and it was linked at that time with United Theological College, Bangalore. After my first year of research in 1999, there was decentralization of doctoral centres and I could shift to FFRRC, Kottayam as my guide was Rev. Dr. M.V. Abraham, who was with FFRRC. The then Registrar of FFRRC, Fr. Dr. K. J. Gabriel (presently Metropolitan Dr Gabriel Mar Gregorios, Trivandrum Diocese of the Orthodox Church) gave me an accommodation near the Orthodox Theological Seminary, and I lived there with my family for the next two years and thus completed my research.

In 2001 the respected Episcopal Synod of the Mar Thoma Church appointed me as a faculty member at the Mar Thoma Seminary. My doctoral vivavoce was held at the Marthoma Seminary Chapel and the external examiners were Dr Dhyanchand Carr from TTS, Madurai and Fr. Dr. John Mathew (a later Registrar of FFRRC and the present Metropolitan, Dr Yuhanon Mar Demetrius of the Delhi Diocese of the Orthodox Church). Without much delay I was awarded the doctoral degree and I could continue my association with FFRRC till date as I have a few scholars doing doctoral research at the FFRRC under my supervision. I deem it a privilege to have taught the M.Th. students of FFRRC for one and half decades. With these words of introduction, I would like to draw our attention to the main topic that I have chosen for this article entitled: **Theological Education in the 21st Century -Some Reflections.**

Theological education could have begun with the inception of the church almost two millennia before. There are over 6000 theological colleges/seminaries/schools/institutes/halls/houses with varying theological emphases and belonging to different church affiliations all over the world today[1]. Most of the well established theological faculties in Western Europe were founded between 14th and 17th centuries (Prague1348; Heidelberg 1386; Oxford 1423; Cambridge 1441; Wittenberg 1502; Marburg 1527; Geneva 1527; Edinburgh 1582). Theological schools in USA and other parts of the world followed: New York 1784; Pittsburgh 1784; Serampore 1818; Caribbean 1830; South Africa Stellenbosch University 1859; Egypt 1859; Hong Kong 1864; Latin America Buenos Aires 1889; Kenya St Paul's UTC 1903; Philippines 1907; UTC, Bangalore 1910; Princeton 1918; Beirut 1932; Jakarta 1934[2]. With these institutions by the early part of the 20th century, the International Missionary Council (IMC) realized that theological education of pastors as well as a general theological education of the lay people especially church workers should be a priority for the churches of the South/two-thirds world. There was also a call for the development of theological education in the vernacular. Of course, indigenous leadership needs theological training in local languages. With these objectives the Theological Education Fund (TEF) was launched in 1958 supported by US and UK mission agencies as well as a major grant from the Rockefeller Foundation. It aimed at Excellence in theological education which included quality (intellectual rigour, spiritual maturity and commitment), authenticity (critical encounter with the local contexts in the design, purpose and shape of theological education), and creativity (promotion of new approaches of the churches in obedience to mission). There was also an emphasis on the development of new curricula for the churches in the South/two-thirds world with new teaching materials written by leading theologians from the South/two-thirds world. The TEF (1958-1977) continued in the form of Program for Theological Education (PTE) since 1977 and as Program for Ecumenical Theological Education (ETE) since 1992 in the World Council of Churches (WCC) to fulfill the Mandate of the TEF in Ministerial Formation. However, the tasks of the TEF have neither been accomplished nor made relevant in changing circumstances.

Despite all efforts at contextualization, some theological seminaries especially the English medium ones in the post-independence era have become kind of elite institutions producing local leaders for church management maintaining the "status quo" instead of creating mission impulses in the community and benefiting the whole people of God in any specific context. In most cases they follow the curriculum that they have inherited. In the case of those theological colleges situated in urban areas, many of the students become urbanized. Thus, relocating them in rural areas becomes a problem with dire consequences sometimes. Hence new patterns of theological education should emerge especially to prepare evangelists, catechists and lay preachers who will cater to the needs of the village congregations and give leadership in rural areas.

Theological Education and Ministerial Formation

The question as to what type of theological education will be more appropriate for mission in the 21st century in a given context is a very important point to be pondered over. Is it "priestly theology" or "pastoral theology" or "prophetic or public theology" that we need for ministry in the church? Or do we need a critical dialogue between theology and other disciplines of science? How does theology for ministerial formation emerge except through indigenization and contextualization?

Theological Education and Christian Mission

It is, nowadays, commonly believed that theological education itself is part of the holistic mission of the church and is therefore missionary in character. Thus theological education should be grounded in worship, which in turn, relates with spirituality, academic excellence, mission and evangelism, justice and peace, pastoral sensitivity and competence as well as in the formation of character. The rediscovery of the missionary nature of the church has a profound impact on the redefining of the missionary task and perspectives of theological education[3]. Mission is to be understood as transforming lives and reconciling communities for mending creation rather than saving souls through conversion into the church.

Theological education should be carried out in partnership with the church, and it should be a relationship of service, ownership and at the same time one of critical distance. As there are different understandings of the Bible, great importance has to be given to biblical hermeneutics in theological education (historical-critical and sociological, charismatic-textual-literal, feminist, Asian and Latin American contextual approaches etc). At the same time theological education should provide an ecumenical perspective for the unity of the church and for interdenominational co-operation. Of course, there needs to be diversity in theological education and the different forms of ministry in the church should be made clear. Therefore, theological education of varying types should be offered for the laity, the deacons, the clergy and bishops. Spiritual formation and missionary training should become part of the programme.

FFRRC has women students, but predominantly from the Baptist churches of North-East India. Not many women from the constituent churches of FFRRC come to study and as a result very few women theologians have emerged through the FFRRC. Theological education should indeed give a greater role to women as half the church membership constitutes of women.

Theological Education in a Plural Religious World

Theological education in the 21st century should respond to religious plurality. Learning about other faiths, equipping the church's ministry with the pastoral capacity to engage positively in inter-faith relations and exploring the fundamental theological pre-suppositions and implications of inter-faith encounter play a very crucial role in this respect[4]. At the level of personal relationships, a growing number of marriages involve couples of different faiths. This has to be tackled at the Christian ministerial and pastoral levels. At a communal level, in some ways it builds relationships of trust and understanding across religious divides and is part of a ministry of reconciliation. Inter-religious encounter is to be seen as part of missiology. Proclamation and dialogue should be part of the church's evangelizing mission. The mission of the church is a sharing in the mission of God. Christian presence among communities of other faiths is the sign of Christ's body of transformation of the society, and of going and receiving hospitality as a sign of the generosity of the Father as revealed through the Trinity.

The Role of theological education in Christian Youth Leadership Formation

Majority of Christians in the South/two-thirds world are young and below forty years of age. Many of the youth are today engaged in Christian communities outside the conventional churches or denominations. In some churches the presence of the young people is diminishing. In many countries churches are desperately in need of young pastors and leadership but not enough people are engaged in theological education.

Children's ministries within Christianity also need to be emphasized. Children are the future of the church. Hence, we need theological education focused on children's and youth ministry today.

Migration and Theological Education

Migration is considered one of the defining global issues of this part of the 21st century as more and more people are on the move today than at any other time in human history. About three percent of the world population (approximately 200 million) people live outside their place of birth. It means that one in 35 persons in the world is a migrant. The current annual growth of migration is about three percent. Hence people should be given special theological training to work among the migrants. In Britain, Germany, USA, Australia, Canada and New Zealand the migrant Christian communities are increasing in number. These diaspora communities have new issues to be faced and theological education should be able to address such issues.

The Relevance of Theological Education for the Unity of the Church

Theological education is a common task for all the churches in the world. Therefore, efforts need to be undertaken in co-operation with other churches. It is indeed a happy thing to note that FFRRC is doing that task at the postgraduate level of theological education in India. There should be more efforts to foster and strengthen interdenominational co-operation.

The Pandemic Covid 19 and the Church Scenario in the World Today

COVID- 19 has changed the mood of the Church in the whole world. A sort of hopelessness and pessimism has crept into many human hearts. Similar situations have affected the world before, but it is in the 21st century that the Church also is in such a predicament. Tens of thousands of active church members including stalwarts in theological education[5] were called to eternity through the pandemic. The Church worldwide must face this dark situation with true courage and abiding hope. She has been the witness to the resurrection of our Lord from the distress and agony of death. It was from the ashes of the theology of death that the theology of hope emerged like the phoenix. The world has survived many plagues, epidemics and world wars. The Spanish flu (1918-20) took away 50 million lives across the globe. AIDS killed 35 million since its inception in 1981. World War II annihilated 70-80 million people (3% of the then world population). COVID-19 may have caused the death of at least 7 million people by now. Those of us who are propelled by the power of the Risen Lord strongly believe that these days of darkness will soon vanish. Hence it is the role of theological educators to keep the beacon of hope burning bright shedding light upon all[6].

The result of a global survey of Christians all over the world may not be very encouraging. In the European countries many huge cathedrals are closing or being sold to be converted into mosques, opera houses or busy malls. In many of the western countries the number of worshippers is dwindling, and churches are unable to maintain their infrastructure and staff. The forecast about the future of the churches there is not very encouraging. However, that is not the full story. In the Sub-Saharan African countries, the churches are growing in leap and bounds. They are not just Pentecostal churches and the charismatic ones, but Anglicans and similar mainline churches. On the Asian side, the Korean churches, though they have cooled down slightly in their international missionary activities of establishing churches all over the world, are flourishing well. Today some of the world's largest churches and congregations are to be found in Korea.

We can take a leaf from the flourishing churches of Africa and Asia, especially from Korea in order to revitalize the rapidly emptying churches of the west. The European and Western churches built huge edifices and cathedrals and invited the community to worship there. These churches were busy enlarging their physical space by making convenient and comfortable infrastructures. In the process they forgot to keep the community attached to the church. In other words, the churches did not get themselves involved in the daily lives and struggles of the people. The church did not accompany the people in their life's journey. In contrast, the African churches emerged out of the community and built themselves in the community not in steeples but in hutments. The community equates itself as the church. The time is at hand when the missionaries from Africa and Asia will have to go to Europe and the North/West to preach to them and evangelize them!

The story of the Church in India is different from that in other countries. The growth of religious fundamentalism and a government which endorses *Hindutva* have become threats to churches in India. The most affected churches are the Pentecostal groups and the independent churches. In the mainline churches of India we see a disappointing trend. These churches have copied the life style of the political parties. The gospel values are replaced by political, partisan and economic values. So, we can see the same type of leadership struggles in the churches also. The unity of early Church is now a forgotten dream. Church leaders, like political leaders, are power centres with money and muscle. A rediscovery of the servant image of our Lord only can redeem the Indian churches[7].

Conclusion

Theological education in the 21st century should take into consideration the present state of the church and the various contexts in which they operate. Hence there cannot be a standard or uniform pattern applicable for all parts of the world and to all the churches. As the contexts differ, some changes are to be made so that there will be adaptability. At the same time the gospel values are never to be sacrificed. The identity of the church as the body of Christ will have to be maintained. As there is only one body for Christ, the various churches should be able to realize themselves as different parts of the same body. The church which is the body of Christ should be controlled by the spirit of the resurrected Jesus Christ.

Women, youth and children need special consideration, and they should be brought to the forefront along with all sections of people who are ostracized from mainstream society. Religious pluralism has to be recognized and tackled in the Christian way. In fact, elements of universalism are to be found in the Bible particularly in the New Testament where we find Jesus dealing with the Samaritan woman, the Roman Centurion, the Syro-Phoenician woman and so on. The Parable of the Good Samaritan (Luke 10) and the Parable of the Last Judgment (Matthew 25) where Jesus divides the people and places them on his right and left in the light of their deeds rather than their birth, should throw light on our theological education in this pluralistic world. Such education should always aim at true excellence which includes quality,authenticity and Creativity. There should also be an emphasis on new curricula development for the churches according to the contexts in the respective regions of the world and new teaching materials written by leading theologians from the concerned regions.

The mission of the church has to be properly tackled and then carried out in different contexts in the most befitting manner as guided by the Holy Spirit. The mission of the church should benefit the whole people of God in any specific context. It is hoped that theological education in the 21st century enable the Church to be a witnessing church.

{*Rev. Dr. Abraham Philip, an ordained priest of the Malankara Marthoma Syrian Church, served as a Professor and Research Guide in the department of New Testament at the Marthoma Theological Seminary and the Federated Faculty for Research in Religion and Culture, (FFRRC) Kottayam. He is a prolific writer and editor. He published many books and articles.*}

Endnotes

[1] Alec Gilmore (ed),*An International Directory of Theological Colleges* (SCM and WCC/ETE, 1997).

[2] Dietrich Werner,*Theological Education in World Christianity* (Program for Theology and Cultures in Asia Series No 2, 2011), 145-49.

[3] David Bosch, "Theological Education in missionary perspective", *Missiology*X/1 (January 1982).

[4] Samuel Amirtham and S Wesley Ariarajah (eds), *Ministerial Formation in a Multi-faith Milieu: Implications for Inter-faith Dialogue for theological education* (Geneva: WCC, 1986).

[5] The Senate of Serampore lost its Registrar, the secretary of the Board of Theological Education, several theological college professors and doctoral research scholars affected by the pandemic.

[6] Rev Dr Ipe Joseph, "From Kuriannur with Love...", *Quo Vadis Ecclesia: Church in the 21st Century- festschrift in honour of Rev Dr M V Abraham: published posthumously*, Editor: Rev Dr Abraham Philip(Tiruvalla: CSS, 2021).

[7] Rev Dr Ipe Joseph, "From Kuriannur with Love...", *Quo Vadis Ecclesia:...*

■■■

Moses-Joshua-Torah: Triad for a Post Pandemic Interpretative World: A Literary Critical Look into the Deuteronomic Admonition in 31:10-13

Fr. Dr. Jacob Mathew

Introduction

It is indeed a privilege to be a literary contributor to the Ruby Volume that is being brought out to mark the milestone of completing forty creative and enriching years of theological learning ecumenically through FFRR. It is even more a surprise and sweet memory for this researcher since he was part of the undergraduate student body at Orthodox Theological Seminary, Kottayam, during the early years of the inception of FFRRC in the 1980s. The frequent visits of teachers from Kerala United Theological Seminary and the off and on presence of teachers like Rev. Dr. K V Mathew and Rev. Dr. M J. Joseph from Mar Thoma Theological Seminary to the Orthodox Theological Seminary, and their close-knit relationship with Metropolitans Mar Paulose Gregorios and Mar Geevarghese Osthathios provided students like me with a newer and wider horizon.[1] This thinking became reinforced when the very same person became part of the academic orbit of FFRRC as student at the level of research programme [DTh], and then as a lecturer in the department of Biblical Studies. It is this feeling of responsibility engendered by the privilege of having been part of the FFRRC that motivates one to look through the final unit of the Book of Deuteronomy and search for a meaningful engagement with the context of the pandemic[2] and post-pandemic world. What follows is a study entitled ***Moses-Joshua-Torah: Triad for a Post Pandemic Interpretive World. A Literary Critical Look into the Deuteronomic Admonition at 31: 10-13.***

Part I

Basics involved in the study:

1. Five blocks of materials in the Book of Deuteronomy

Following Daniel L. Christensen,[3] the structure of the Book of Deuteronomy could be described in terms of a five-part concentric design with the following materials:

i. Retrospective material contained in chs. 1-3,

ii. Exhortative material in chs. 4-11,

iii. Central core of the book presented in chs. 12-26 [covenant stipulations],

iv. The covenant ceremony in chs.27-30,

v. Forward looking document with a note on the death of its leader in chs. 31–34.

Out of these five blocks of materials, the forward-looking document contained in chs. 31-34, particularly a selected portion of ch 31 [vv. 10-13] is the matter of interest here.

2. Unique Oration in Deut Ch. 31.

i. **Distinct stylistic narrative:** In the final discourse of Moses [Deut29:1- 34:12], which begins with a summary narration on the covenant ceremony [ch.29], Chapter 31 has a space in the actualization of the covenant ceremony and the succession of Joshua. Presented in a distinct narrative style of its own, ch. 31 narrates how Moses gravely describes his imminent exit from the scene [vv.1-6], the divine selection of Joshua to lead the people of God thereafter [vv.7-8], the transferring of Torah from oral existence to written form [vv.9-13], the final words of Moses and an introduction to the song of Moses [vv.14- 30]. Chapter 31is to be particularly noted for its stylistically formulated orations touching upon the transition in leadership, status, form and significance of Torah, inclusive perspective, invitation to tread with vigour and commitment in their journey, endowing of three successors to Moses and a newer emphasis on the fear of Lord.

ii. **Militant but Inclusive; Sober yet speaks of the Triad:** The segment of valedictory oration[4] in Deut. Ch. 31 is created in the style of 'Military orations'[5] which we come across frequently in the retrospective and exhortative admonitions of Book of Deuteronomy.[6]Transfer of leadership and the depositing of Torah as Witness is the topic under discussion in Deuteronomy 31:1-29. In vv. 14-16, God tells Moses directly that he is about to die, but Israel has to pursue its journey to the Promised Land. As per the discourse, no one, not even Moses, can claim superior authority. Instead, with the word of God being given out as witness and as the normative command, the entire Israelite community in the most inclusive definition of its identity, must tread forward and continuously open itself to new situations. When Moses departs God provides them, in effect with 'three successors to Moses': Joshua, the written Torah and a poem to consider.[7] Even though Moses departs, his unseen presence will be felt with the written Torah, Joshua and with the all encompassing presence of the Lord. In that manner, the Triad is redefined as comprising Moses-Joshua and the Torah. In other words, everything is focused towards the written Torah and the divine presence.

iii. **Transfer of authority and a newer perspective:** The passage [31:9-13[8]]indicates a transfer of authority at a newer level. Just as the beginning of that chapter places transfer of the leadership role of Moses to Joshua, it is directed that the oral word of Moses should give way for the "book" form of Torah. They are instructed to read it aloud periodically before all Israel (vv. 10-11). Not only that, the written Torah is to be a directive principle for the people of God forever in their life, it is to be with a new perspective: an inclusive perspective[9] with deserving space for "all Israel" (v. 11) including 'men, women, children, and the foreigners residing in their towns' (v. 12).

iv. **Renewed emphasis on "fear of the Lord"**[v.12]: Fear of the Lord as visualized by "all Israel" is given out with a special emphasis. As noted under point iii above, it is to be observed by all including the foreigners residing there irrespective of their gender or other identities. What is implied is not simply the observance of certain of the stipulations of a spiritualized piety,on the other hand universal morality or "general morality"[10]is implied. The admonition regarding fear of the Lord ['irathAdonai,'Hb] has also to be seen in the backdrop of Deut 25:18, where it is not at all linked with Yhwh, nor has it 'any national limitations.'[11] If that 'fear' could be linked in the pre-deuteronomic period with an unprotected stranger [Gen20: 11] or with the Hebrew midwives [Ex1:17] or with an

Israelite in exile [Gen42:18], the Deuteronomic admonition to fear the Lord "all of one's days" [31: 13] gets a fresh spurt.[12]

Part II

Instructions for a new beginning

3. **Instructions Appropriate to the Divine Presence**: Immediately following the analysis of humbled status [31:1-2] where Moses confided that his advanced age has incapacitated him and the shock at the Lord informing him that 'he shall not cross over Jordan'has weakened him [31:2], Moses gave instructions first to "the children of Israel" and then particularly to the leader who is succeeding him [31:7ff.]. The instructions which are spread all though the sub-unit has the typical Deuteronomic flavour[13]in content and phraseology. The text then states about the writing down of the Torah [31:9] which furthers the instructions. The crux of the instructions on the basis of the reading of the Torah has a bearing upon the life of the people of God in 'all the days of their life.' It requires them to have a newer understanding of commitment for a renewed life in their ongoing journey. The **instruction** apparently **has four elements** appropriate to the status of continuing in the guaranteed presence of the Lord. The four elements are:

    a. **Gather with a renewed appointment:**Just in comparison to the focus on Tabernacle or appointed place ['ohelmoed,' Heb.] to meet the Lord, here is an invitation to restructure [historical] time period for an appointment with the Lord: *time for a fresh gathering with a renewed appointment*. The context for appointment though stated with reference to the 'year of Remission and the feast of Tabernacles' [v. 10] is an invitation to focus on that time ['appointed time' or 'moediim,' Heb] for the organization of life. It provides a structure for differentiating between the temporary and the permanent [or continuous] awareness of presence of the Lord. The people of the Lord, in their journey had to face a lot of struggles, insecurities at multifarious levels, loss of life et al. The appointment of Joshua is to equip them to face future dangers in the absence of the guidance and intervention of Moses, who had led them through all the trials they had faced until then. It is in the midst of this temporary and fragile protection of Moses that a permanent solution is offered, viz.,the continuous presence of the Divine Providence. Even then there is an invitation to redefine their lives by gathering for a renewed appointment which may involve the other three aspects discussed below. Those aspects should consider **life** to be **one of continuous seeking** rather **than one that should be viewed with certitude.**

b. **Be renewed with curiosity to learn and impart the Torah**: Perhaps more significantly placed in the text than the appointment of Joshua, is the *allegiance to the Torah*, which is 'to be read and heard' [v.12]. This provides the mode of the placement of the Torah in the lives of the people in transition; gathering of the people at the appointed place of meeting and their allegiance to the Torah in the course of their whole life are closely related with each other. To quote from an author from a different context of analysis, 'Torah emerges as a crucial constant in the face of changing circumstances.'[14]Learning and imparting the message of Torah is significant. This is more so because when Moses departs and Joshua takes charge, the supremacy of Yahweh is firmly established: 'all the people to appear before the presence of the Lord [v. 11] and with utmost allegiance to the Torah. It is as if Torah offers the standard by which people should live and step forth in their journey[v.13], and the life of the people of God should be in utmost loyalty to the Torah. It is presumed that the Torah alone could compensate for the lost presence of Moses. Only the Torah can help fulfill the expectations of the people and enable them experience the presence of the Lord.

c. **Refined inculcation and renewed with "fear of the Lord**:"The community is addressed to promote an inculcation along the lines of fear of God: to feel the real presence of the Lord in their midst all through their lives. As we know, 'ir at Adonai'[Heb] is not in any way directly linked with what is generally being said as 'piety' as such, rather it points to a sense of 'awe before the Lord' [vv. 12-13], a regular and continuous feeling of the presence of the Lord. The other part of inculcation is to have an inclusive perspective with a broader understanding of "all Israel" including "men, women, children and the aliens." No doubt the invitation is for the genuine application of Torah to personal and societal life.

d. **Re-established with renewed commitment:** The admonition to fear the Lord "all of one's days" [31: 13], is a demand for committed response in the perceivable future of the historical person and for all generations to come [cp. Deut6:6]. Since the generation listening to the valedictory speech made to Moab and the "sons" who "cross over the Jordan to inherit" [v.13b] is to have allegiance to the Lord through their adherence to the Torah, it has bearing on every people in transition.

Just like the journeying people of Moab, those who live in the period of the pandemic also are in a period of transition during which the security-even the feeling of safety-, prosperity and wellness of the people are severely affected. The leaders and the ordinary people, the citizens of every country and their diaspora, men, women and children have all been affected. But all those who passed through this turmoil and survived, need to renew their commitment to the Leader, the Lord and the Torah in "all of one's days."

Life in transition is life with limitations. Nevertheless, since life and living have to move forward in all fullness Life demands total commitment. It is not life as such that is affected in a pandemic situation rather what is affected are the amenities of life. The people in transition need to move ahead with the awareness that, it is not Life that is being put into confinement or quarantine, but only the physical elements of it. Life in transition might be provided with the necessary backing which is presented in the text as *the Triad* to lead in the presence of the Lord.

Conclusion

The pandemic has to be faced and the post pandemic situations have to be managed with an openness to the situation of people in transition. There are struggles related to the loss of security and togetherness, problems of confinement and the trauma of death. The leader and the led may be lost in the feeling of being deprived of all that had until then been taken for granted. They must face the quite unexpected loss of an atmosphere congenial to life as well the great sorrow of losing loved ones. But accepting the Triad of Moses-Joshua-Torah and the empowerment of the presence of the Lord, the society could move forward. This move forward is expected to be with a feeling of inclusiveness. This way, the text provides an interpretive solution to face realities; life needs to be lived in seeking along with all Israel. In the inclusivity promoted in the text, there is no space for any kind of certitude, but only that obtained by seeking the presence of the Lord. *Torah as the revealed will of the Lord* should be searched to promote an inculcation along the lines of fear of God: to feel His real presence in their midst all through their lives.

{Fr. Dr. Jacob Mathew, an ordained priest of the Malankara Orthodox Syrian Church, serving as a Professor and Research Guide in the department of Old Testament at the Orthodox Theological Seminary and the Federated Faculty for Research in Religion and Culture, (FFRRC) Kottayam. He wrote certain devotional books and two secular fictions in Malayalam.}

Endnotes

[1] The three supporting seminaries of FFRRC viz Kerala United Theological Seminary of the Church of South India, Marthoma Theological Seminary of the Marthoma Church, Orthodox Theological Seminary of the Orthodox Syrian Church.

[2] By Pandemic we mean the [Corona] virus induced widespread serious health issues, unexpected casualties, and the subsequent containment situation that affected all the aspects of normal life and existence in the world in a very critical manner in the years 2020 and 2021. On 11 March 2020, World Health Organization characterized COVID-19 as "a pandemic" that created "a global public health emergency."

[3] Daniel L. Christensen.*Deuteronomy 1-11*, Word Biblical Commentary Series, Vol. 6A (Dallas, Texas: Word Books, 1991), XLI. This division follows Julius Wellhausen (who earlier held the view that Deut. Chs. 1-4 & 5-11 was two introductions to Deut. 12-26):*Prolegomena to the History of Ancient Israel.* 1885. (New York: The Word Publishing Company, 1961), 369.

[4] The Book of Deuteronomy as such being presented as a valedictory oration by Moses.

[5] The 'Military orations' as identifiable from Deut. Chs. 1,2,7,9,11 and further in Ch.31 are presented as if a person of priestly responsibilities delivers some inspiring words in the form of a speech to the Israelite warriors prior to their departure for battle.Moshe Weinfeld, *Deuteronomy and the Deuteronomic School*, 45.

[6] The valedictory oration of Book of Deuteronomycontains distinct stylistic orations like Liturgical orations, Prophetic orations and Military orations. Moshe Weinfeld, *Deuteronomy and the Deuteronomic School*, 10-58. This opinion is in continuation to what G. von Rad presented in his pioneering work Studies in Deuteronomy, 78ff.

[7] Stephen L. Cook, *Reading Deuteronomy: A Literary and Theological Commentary,* [Macon, GA : Smyth &Helwys Publishing, 2014], 225.

[8] and later at vv. 24-27.

[9] Stephen L. Cook, *Reading Deuteronomy: A Literary and Theological Commentary,*226.

[10] Moshe Weinfeld, *Deuteronomy and the Deuteronomic School,* 274.It is interesting to note with Moshe Weinfeld that both in the Torah particularly in the book of Deuteronomy and in the Wisdom literature 'covenant fidelity'has a compatible treatment along the lines of 'general morality.' Part III of the book deals extensively with this. Moshe Weinfeld, *Deuteronomy and the Deuteronomic School,* 244-316.

[11] Moshe Weinfeld, *Deuteronomy and the Deuteronomic School,* 274.

[12] This goes quite in line with *beacharithhayyamim* of Deut.31:29, which is rendered as a time not far in the future rather days in the perceivable future of the historical person. Analysis along this line is available with Willis John T, [The Expression *beacharithhayyamin* in the Old Testament, *Restoration Quarterly,* 22 no 1 – 2. 1979], 58. [pp.54-71].

[13] The Deueteronomic thinking as perceived by scholars is not simply subscribing to the ideas of the book of Deuteronomy.Rather an ideological reflection of the spirit of the times of its compilation in carefully crafted phraseology,and along the basic tenets related to Exodus, Covenant, Election, Inheritance of Land, Loyalty to the Torah et al. Accordingly, YHWH demands unconditional allegiance to the Torah. Disloyalty to the Torah accrues punishment and removal from the land, repentance and loyalty will cause return to the Land.This is extensively being dealt by Moshe Weinfeld (Deuteronomy and the Deuteronomic School) and Raymond F. Brown, *The Deuteronomic School: History, Social Setting, and Literature* [Atlanta, Society for Biblical Literature, 2002],19-20, 104-106. To Weinfeld, the book of Deuteronomy has to be seen against the backdrop of a strong sapiential tradition; i.e. to the sages of the royal court of Judah during the eight and seventh centuries Bc.

[14] Peter T. Vogt. *Deuteronomic Theology and the Significance of Torah : A Reappraisal* [Indiana, Eisenbrauns, 2006], 111.

■■■

Matthean Account of Jesus' Ministry: Implications for Christian Ministry in the COVID Pandemic

Rev. Dr. Koshy P. Varughese

1. Introduction

While reading the synoptic gospels, one finds that Jesus has a special care and concern for the downtrodden, the lost, the burdened, the little ones, the poor and the humble. This is most strongly presented in the Gospel of Matthew. The synoptic gospels report the beginning of Jesus' ministry differently. Mark narrates the beginning of Jesus' public ministry as "Now after John was arrested, Jesus came to Galilee, proclaiming the good news of God"(Mk 1:14). Luke reports, "Then Jesus, filled with the power of the Spirit, returned to Galilee, and a report about him spread through all the surrounding country. He began to teach in their synagogues and was praised by everyone" (Lk 4:14-15). Matthew edited Mark's statement of facts and added a quotation of his own, "Now when Jesus heard that John had been arrested, he withdrew to Galilee....so that what had been spoken through the prophet Isaiah might be fulfilled: ...the people who sat in darkness have seen a great light, and for those who sat in the region and shadow of death light has dawned"(Mt 4:12-16).Jesus' withdrawal to Galilee is not for safety purposes. Hans-Reudi Weber says, "He did not go where the important people lived, to Jerusalem or Caesarea. Jesus withdrew in to the "Galilee of the Gentiles" – a highly suspect and rather backward area in the eyes of those who counted in Jerusalem. There he fulfilled Isaiah's prophecy"[1]. Warren Carter writes, "Jesus withdraws into a dangerous situation created by John's arrest, in which he will now carry out God's purposes".[2]Galilee was a Roman occupied territory and also geographically distant from and marginal to hostile Jerusalem. Warren Carter says that Galilee symbolizes "the periphery (which becomes) the new, non-localized center of divine presence." This shows that by using this quotation Matthew intends to show the special care of Jesus for the people who are burdened, poor, downtrodden, lost etc. This paper is an attempt to locate the ministry of Jesus in the Matthean narrative and the implication it has in the Christian ministry especially during the Covid pandemic.

2. Jesus' Ministry of Preaching/Teaching and Healing

Matthew summarizes the content of Jesus' ministry as preaching / teaching and healing (Mt 4:23; 9:35). In these two summaries of Jesus' ministry, the words are almost identical and offer the image of Jesus wandering about cities and villages, carrying out his ministry of teaching/ preaching and healing. Mt 9:36 says, "When he saw the crowds, he had compassion for them, because they were harassed and helpless, like sheep without a shepherd." This verse traces the reasons for Jesus' ceaseless activity to his compassion for the crowds who are like "sheep without a shepherd". "Compassion" is the hallmark of Jesus' character (Mt 14:14; 15: 32; 18: 27; 20: 34). Jesus had compassion for these people who are exploited and are like sheep without a shepherd.[3] The expression "sheep without a shepherd' refers to the marginalized people of the

Jewish community. The Galileans were considered as second-class Jews. The tax- collectors were considered as outcasts. The women were considered as "excluded people" in the Jewish community. The lame, the blind and the deaf were considered unfit to enter the temple. The people with leprosy were totally ostracized. These were the people who were sheep without a shepherd.[4] Matthew portrays that Jesus' ministry enhances the life of these weak and oppressed people. Jesus was touched by the masses because they were leaderless, harassed and helpless.

2.1. Reversal of conditions for the distressed (Mt 5:3-12)

In the Beatitudes, Jesus who is to shepherd God's people now promises eschatological salvation. The poor, the mournful, the meek etc., whom Jesus addresses in the beatitudes are those who have nothing to expect from the world, but who survive in their expectation and hope for a new age. The common factor which unites all the addressees in the beatitudes, is their hope for the new age with reversal of values has dawned through the ministry of Jesus. G. Bornkamm expresses this fact as follows:

> What unites those addressed in the beatitudes and pronounced blessed, is this, that they are driven to the very end of the world and its possibilities; the poor, who do not fit into the structure of the world and therefore are rejected by the world; the mourners, for whom the world holds no consolation; the humble, who long to extract recognition from the world; the hungry and thirsty who cannot live without the righteousness that God alone can promise and provide in this world. But also the merciful, who without asking about rights, open their hearts to another; the peacemakers, who overcome might and power by reconciliation; the righteous, who are not equal to the evil ways of the world; and finally the persecuted, who with scorn and threat of death, are cast bodily out by the world.[5]

The divine passive in the second member of the beatitudes makes clear that God is the unexpressed subject of the action ("will be comforted", "will be filled", "will receive mercy", "will be called children of God"- in all these, God is the understood agent).[6] This means that the eschatological hope for the new age has become an experience in the "now" of the ministry of Jesus. Jesus, who earlier announced that the kingdom of heaven has come near (4:17), now through these beatitudes proclaims salvation in the form of an eschatological reversal of conditions for the people who are in distress. He calls his hearers "blessed' because they are to experience God's compassion and inherit the new kingdom. These beatitudes are not just announcements, but in the messianic ministry of Jesus, these blessings of the new age have dawned.[7] Jesus, the King, became a medium of messianic justice and peace to those who are depressed and seek liberation through his servant ministry. The eschatological salvation of the poor has become a reality in and through the ministry of Jesus. The kingdom of heaven is offered to the poor in their helplessness through the ministry of Jesus. The blessedness of the kingdom reaches to them through Jesus and thus reveals the nature of God's rule in the kingdom which he proclaims and represents. D. Hill rightly says that the beatitudes express the newness that God makes possible in the life and ministry of Jesus.[8]

2.2. Mercy to the sinners and tax collectors

Jesus' table fellowship with the sinners and tax collectors is an expression of this eschatological salvation, which was promised to the poor, the hungry and the mourning.[9] This eschatological salvation brought by Jesus, shows mercy to the sinners and tax collectors. The sinners and tax –collectors who were considered as outcasts began to receive mercy and forgiveness. Jesus associated with them and ate with them. Marcus J. Borg describes Jesus' table fellowship with tax collectors and sinners "as one of the most conspicuous and controversial aspects of the renewal movement founded by him."[10] The "central feature" of Jesus' messianic ministry may be his table fellowship with tax collectors and sinners.[11] The "sinners and tax- collectors" were a category of people despised by the Jewish people. Jesus' attitude to them was different from that of the contemporary Jewish religion. Matthew records messianic Jesus' association with the tax collectors and sinners and the criticisms leveled against Jesus. In Mt 9:10f. (Mk 2:15f; Lk 5: 29-30), Matthew shows that Jesus is eating with many tax collectors and sinners at the house of Matthew, the tax collector, whom he has called to follow him. The purity- conscious religious leaders of his people resent this table fellowship criticizing Jesus for eating with the tax collectors and sinners. In this context of Pharisaic criticism of Jesus' associating with the sinners, Jesus makes clear the very nature of his kingly ministry, "For I have come to call not the righteous but sinners." The name "Jesus" means "Saviour" (Mt 1: 21). The nature of the kingly rule of God is revealed in his words and actions. The messianic, forgiving love of God has dawned in Jesus' ministry. This is very evident in Matthew's adding of Jesus' saying, "I desire mercy, not sacrifice" (Mt 9:13; 12:7). Of all the gospel writers, only Matthew quotes Hosea's words about mercy. These same words from Hosea is repeated in Mt 12:7 also where it is an answer to the Pharisees who criticized Jesus' disciples for violating the Sabbath by plucking heads of grain (Mt 12:1-8). Jesus' reply points out the fact that "God is no longer primarily understood as the demanding one, but as the gracious one, the merciful one."[12] Michael Crosby says, "...Matthew shows the leaders of Jewish religion are not able to move beyond their legalism to bend the law to meet human needs."[13] This promise of the blessings of the kingdom of heaven becomes a reality to those who are outcast and needy. Thus, the sinners and the defenseless meet a merciful Saviour in Jesus.

2.3. Not burden imposing, but burden lifting

Matthew portrays Jesus as one who offers rest to those "who are weary and burdened" (Mt 11:28-30). Mt 11: 27 projects the uniqueness and authority of Jesus as the Son of the Father to whom "all things have been handed over by the Father". A similar statement is further made in Mt 28:18 by the resurrected Christ who commissions the disciples for mission, "... all authority in heaven and on earth has been given to me". These point to the unique position of Jesus as the mediator of the knowledge of God to humankind and reveal the identity of Jesus as the unique representative of God.[14] Based on this authority handed over to him, Jesus, the authoritative Son of God, invites the "weary and the burdened" to come to him and take his yoke, which guarantees the promised rest (Mt 11: 28-30). The "weary and the burdened" probably refers to those suffering under the burdens imposed by the Pharisaic establishment.[15] They presently labor under an encumbering load from which they can only find rest if they take up the new yoke of the Son.

The authoritative Son exercises his authority in meekness and gentleness and provides the eschatological rest to the weak and rejected.[16]Jesus' statement, "my yoke is easy and my burden is light" does not mean that he makes lighter demands. Jesus' yoke is "easy" which normally means "kind", "comfortable" not because it makes lighter demands, but because it represents entering into a master-disciple relationship ("learn from me") with one who is gentle and humble in heart.[17] This means that, unlike the Pharisees Jesus does not lay the law as a burden on people and then withdraws and condemns people for their failure to keep it. Jesus is not a demanding taskmaster, nor is he a stern arbiter requiring perfection from the hands of peoples. He is, rather, the messenger of God's saving work, the full expression of God's mercy.[18] The yoke of Jesus is not burdensome, instead it is characterized by humility and concern for the outcasts.[19] Thus, Matthew presents Jesus, who does not use his power to coerce but to enhance the life of the rejected people. Thus, the ministry of Jesus was not burden imposing but burden lifting.[20]

2.4. Healing Jesus

Matthew's two summary statements of Jesus' acts of healing (Mt 8:16; Mt 12:15-16) are succeeded by two formula quotations from the servant songs of Isaiah (Mt 8:17= Isa 53:4; Mt 12:18-21= Isa 42;1-4). Mt 8:1-15 describes the healing of three "excluded persons" from the Jewish point of view. They are a leper, the servant of a centurion and a woman (Peter's mother-in-law). This is followed by the summary of Jesus' acts of healing which is succeeded by the formula quotation from the Servant song of Isaiah 53:4 in Mt 8:17. By using this formula quotation, Matthew depicts the healing miracles of Jesus as the fulfillment of what had been told by the prophet. Though the text of Isaiah 53 speaks about the Servant who brings healing to people through his own suffering and dying for sins, Matthew has used this text of Isaiah 53 in order to project the servant ministry of Jesus. Birger Gerhardson rightly points out that the primary function of the quotation from Isaiah 53 in Mt 8:17 is Christological and he says, "the prophetic words and the evangelist's portrayal of Jesus do, however, coincide on a crucial point: the "Servant" frees the people from disease".[21] Matthew tries to show that Jesus who heals is the Servant of God. This means that miracles of Jesus flow from his mercy and meekness. Jesus is not self-serving, rather he identifies with the suffering humanity and uses his power for the weak. By quoting Isaiah 42:1-4 in Mt 12:18-21, Matthew again projects the character of the kingly ministry of Jesus who heals, and draws further attention to the meekness (v.19), the gentleness (v.20) and the ultimate goal of His work (justice to the Gentilesv.18, 20, 21). The saving activities of Jesus resemble those of Isaiah's Servant, whose mission is to bring relief and comfort to the needy and the unfortunate (cf. Isa 42:7). He has compassion upon all, especially the weak and vulnerable, symbolized by the "bruised reed" or "smoking wick." This quotation again reminds us of the previous passages which depict Jesus as helping the "harassed and helpless" (Mt 9:35) and the "weary and burdened" (Mt 11:28).

Whereas Mark has only three "Son of David" references, Matthew has nine and of the nine references, except for those outside the infancy narrative, all "Son of David" references in Matthew are used in relation with the healing acts of Jesus. All those who were healed by the " Son of David" are persons who in the eyes of the contemporary Jewish society, count for nothing or as J. D. Kingsbury labels them "the no- accounts" of the society (" two blind men, 9:27; 20:30; the " blind and lame" in the Temple, 21:14; a " blind and dumb man," 12:22; and a " daughter" who is demon possessed, 15:22).[22] Thus, the story of the Son of David in Matthew is not the story of war but it is the story of the liberation of the simple people. In Matthew's account of Jesus' entry into Jerusalem (Mt 21:1-16), Jesus is depicted as the Son of David who is humble and meek. One of the references to the Son of David who heals is presented in this pericope. Thus, Matthew brings the theme of Jesus as King (Son of David) entering the city of Jerusalem not as a military conqueror but as a peaceful healer. Jesus, the Davidic king is different from the kings of the Old Testament, he comes not as a warrior king but as one who is meek and humble as the Servant of Yahweh and heals the people. W. Carter says that the reign of God which was revealed through Jesus' ministry of preaching and healing, unlike the many Judean kings, was "life- giving, not death- bringing" and it was committed to bring justice to the poor and needy (Ps 72; Mt 5-9).[23] In Jesus the real goal of kingship was manifested, that is the well-being of God's people (1Kings 3: 8-9) not the glory of the king. So, Jesus the King uses his power for the weak and the oppressed.

3. Implication of the study

Our study made clear that the Matthean Jesus' ministry of preaching/teaching and healing is not an authoritarian one but an enhancing one. It enhances the lives of the distressed, the poor, the burdened, the downcast, the lost, despised, the weak and the defenseless etc. Two years have passed since the pandemic was declared a universal disaster, but the crisis is still wreaking havoc and growing at a rapid rate. One can expect that COVID-19 virus will be around in some form or the other for the next few years, impacting human lives in different ways. It is not possible to presume that we will return to a pre-covid era, but it is almost certain that life situations will take us to new levels of understanding concerning humanity, religion and society. The pandemic resulted in the visibility of trauma symptoms amongst individuals and communities due to the loss of safe assumptions about the stability of the world and human existence. We are seeing the manifestations of this in such new normal practices like social distancing as well as disruption of everyday life, pain and sorrow, emotional trauma, anxiety and stress. Such practices lead to greater awareness and attentiveness to new perspectives regarding ministry needs. This calls for the church to be active in ministry being proactive rather than passive in their response to trauma and loss. People are seeking desperately for an anchor of spiritual sustenance- searching for meaning in the midst of futility and uncertainty, searching for God, reaching out for a firm foothold where the earth is moving, searching to discover and to understand who God is in their lives. The sheer scale of human suffering, brokenness, hurt, pain, and suffering are bound to draw men and women of faith into searching and seeking for meaning in the midst of the futility that envelops them. The full horror of the human degradation will never be fully comprehended. It is at times like these that people will be drawn to the substance of their faith.

The *Arusha Call to Discipleship* is pertinent here[24]. It is the Final Statement of the World Council of Churches' Conference on World Mission and Evangelism, "Moving in the Spirit: Called to Transforming Discipleship," held in Tanzania 8–13 March 2018. The statement makes a compelling case that Christians are called to faithful discipleship, learners at the feet of Christ, discoverers of the truth about Christ and the World. It says forcefully that "discipleship is both a gift and a call to be active collaborators with God for the transforming of the world (1 Thessalonians 3:2)." In our study, we saw that in the Matthean understanding discipleship in Christian ministry is a call to have compassion on people and to lead the communities in hope and faith. (Mt.9:36). This journey of discipleship is an invitation to the churches to serve the world by affirming life and by their commitment to bring justice to the poor and needy. Thus, we are responding to Jesus' call to follow him from the margins of the world.

The church as a transforming and reconciling community seeks in its life to manifest the salvation of the world and the glorification of God the Father in its life and work. As a moral exemplar of Christ in the world the church needs to serve as a reconciling agent between God and society, bringing hope and healing to all those who are distressed, suffering and the marginalized as Jesus offers rest to those "who are weary and burdened" (Mt 11:28-30).

{Rev. Dr. Koshy P. Varughese is the former Principal of Dharma Jyoti Vidya Peeth Seminary, Faridabad and the first registrar of Nav Jyoti Post Graduate Research Centre, New Delhi. Currently he serves as the Professor and research guide in the department of New Testament at Mar Thoma Theological Seminary and FFRRC, Kottayam and serves as the registrar of FFRRC, Kottayam.}

Endnotes

[1] Hans-Reudi Weber, *The Invitation, Matthew on Mission* (New York: Joint Commission on Education and Cultivation, Board of Missions of the United Methodist Church, 1971),34.

[2] Warren Carter, *Matthew and the Margins: A Socio-Political and Religious Reading*, The Bible & Liberation Series(Mary knoll, New York: Orbis Books, 2001),113.

[3] D. A. Carson, *When Jesus Confronts the World: An Exposition of Matthew 8-10* (Grand Rapids, Michigan: Baker Book House, 1987), 111-112.

[4] Dhyanchand Carr, *Sword of the Spirit: An Activist's Understanding of the Bible*, RBS (Geneva: WCC, 1992), 47.

[5] G. Bornkamm, *Jesus of Nazareth*, Translated by Irene and Fraser McLuskey and James M. Robinson (London: Hodder &Stoughton, 1988),76.

[6] J. P. Meier, *The Vision of Matthew*, 35. In order to avoid using the name of God, passive voice was used by Jewish people, that is why divine passive: see M. E. Boring, "The Gospel of Matthew," in *The New Interpreter's Bible*, Vol.8, edited by Leander E. Keck et al., (Nashville: Abingdon Press, 1995), 179.

[7]Koshy P. Varughese, *King-Servant Christology in Matthew's Gospel* (New Delhi: ISPCK,2013),88.

[8] D. Hill, *Matthew*, N C B C (Grand Rapids, Michigan: William B. Eerdmans Publishing Company, 1990),110.

[9] U. Luz, *Matthew 1-7*, A Commentary, Translated by Wilhelm C. Linss (Minneapolis: Fortress Press, 1985),231.

[10] Marcus J. Borg, *Conflict, Holiness & Politics in the Teachings of Jesus: Studies in the Bible and Early Christianity*, vol.5 (New York, The Edwin Mellen Press, 1984), 78-79.

[11] Norman Perrin, *Re-discovering the Teaching of Jesus* (London: SCM, 1967), 107.

[12] Gerhard Barth, "Matthew's Understanding of the Law," in G nther Bornkamm, Gerhard Barth and Heinz Joachim Held, *Tradition and Interpretation in Matthew* (London, SCM Press,1963), 83.

[13] Michael H. Crosby, *Spirituality of the Beatitudes: Matthew's Challenge for First World Christians* (Maryknoll, New York: Orbis Books, 1981), 143.

[14] Donald A. Hagner, *Matthew 1-13*, W B C, vol. 33A (Texas: Word Books, 1993), 320.

[15] B. Charette, "To Proclaim Liberty to the Captives: Matthew 11:28-30 in the Light of Prophetic Expectation" *New Testament Studies* 38/ 2 (April, 1992): 294f.

[16] W. D Davies and Dale C. Allison, Jr. *A Critical and Exegetical Commentary on the Gospel According to Saint Matthew* Vol.2 (Edinburgh: T. & T. Clark, 1991), 288-289.

[17] R. T. France, *The Gospel According to Matthew: An Introduction and Commentary*, Re-printed (Leicester, England: InterVarsity Press, 1992), 201.

[18] Donald Verseput, *The Rejection of the Humble Messianic King: A Study of the Composition of Matthew* 11-12 (Frankfurt: Peter Lang, 1986),151.

[19] David Hill, *The Gospel of Matthew*,208.

[20] Brendan Byrne, Lifting the Burden-Reading Matthew's Gospel in the Church Today (Collegeville, Minnesota: Liturgical Press, 2004).

[21] Birger Gerhardson, *The Mighty Acts of Jesus According to Matthew*, Translated by Robert Dewsnap (Lund: CWK Gleerup, 1979), 25.

[22] J. D. Kingsbury, "The Title 'Son of David' in Matthew's Gospel," *Journal of Biblical Literature* 95 / 4 (December, 1978): 599.

[23] W. Carter, *Matthew and the Margins: A Socio-Political and Religious Reading*, The Bible & Liberation Series(Mary knoll, New York: Orbis Books, 2001), 234.

[24] World Council of Churches, The Arusha Call to Discipleship, 13 March 2018, https://www.oikoumene.org/resources/documents/the-arusha-call-to-discipleship.

■■■

Authority in the Church: Re Envisioning the Thought of Dr. Paulos Gregorios

Fr. Dr. Ninan K George

Introduction

The blessed memory of Dr. Paulos Mar Gregorios (PMG), an eminent philosopher and a renowned theologian who lived in the Malankara (Indian) Orthodox Syrian Church paves the way for numerous memoirs to those who are fortunate to experience his overwhelming scholarship in different spheres of learning. I myself was privileged to have been part of different sessions led by His Grace at the BD and M.Th. level of theological pursuit. He was one of the leading pioneers who took the initiative in having a common theological platform i.e., FFRRC, Kottayam, for three church traditions - Orthodox, Mar Thoma and Church of South India (CSI). It is a coincidence that the Malankara Orthodox Church celebrates the 25th death anniversary of His Grace Paulos Mar Gregorius of blessed memory and the FFRRC celebrates its Ruby Year in 2021. This article is my humble tribute based on one of the theological works of His Grace Paulos Mar Gregorius of blessed memory.

Authority an Introduction

Dr. Paulos Mar Gregorius took the initiative to explain Authority in circumstances that were misunderstood by people who promoted volitional authority – authority as control of one's will by another's and submission to another's decisions.[1] According to him authority is suspect in both its forms-accepting some statement or conclusion on the authority of others, or submitting oneself to obedience and control by others. In order to provide the proper orientation on this concept, he upheld the Septuagint term *exousia* or *epitage* and elucidated its meaning as follows:

> It means primarily the ability to be a subject and not an object, to act, not to be acted upon, to make things and people obey you, to achieve something, to have power, skill and ability within oneself, to be acting out of one's own free motion and not by compulsion.[2]

The Concise Theological Dictionary offers one definition of authority:

> (Authority is) the palpable, demonstrable trustworthiness or legal claim of a person ... capable of convincing another person of some truth or of the validity of a command and obliging him to accept it, even though that truth or valid character is not immediately evident. The acceptance of a command on authority is called obedience; the similarly motivated acceptance of a truth is called faith. Both are modes of indirect recognition based on the authority of an intermediary.

It is a fact that nothing is exempted from living under various forms of authority. The bishop says, "Neither science nor religion can function without authority. No single scientist can start from scratch and prove everything for himself. He accepts the authority of the scientific community for most of knowledge."[3]In the age of democratic liberty in which we live, nobody is interested of "being managed" by someone else. Everybody wants freedom from authority. But since we are citizens of this world or a particular country which has its own constitutions and cultures, we have to obey the laws of the State and concludes that "there can neither be knowledge nor common life without some form of authority."[4]

Authority in the Church

Regarding the role of authority (intellectual authority that is used for making statements and volitional authority that is used to control one's will by another's) in the life of Church is also same as of other functioning of the world. Dr. Paulos Mar Gregorius says, "It is a community with its own mind and its own way of relating within itself and with others."[5]He was very much interested in studying on how that authority is structured for the meaningful witness of the church in the world. When one deals with the purpose of authority in the church, the authority of God cannot be overlooked.

St. Paul teaches that God is the source spring of all authority as he exhorted in his letter to the Romans.[6]The bishop continues, "Authority of God is His freedom – to be what He wills to be. He wills what He is and is what He wills. His will becomes reality. And that is both true freedom and true authority."[7] He deliberates that human beings are made in the image of God; humanity has been given freedom and authority which God respects.[8] According to him the 'image of God' is the source of dignity of the human- this respect of God for the freedom He has bestowed upon everyone.[9]This is the factor that makes the great church fathers to exhort on 'obedience' the virtue which inspires us to grow in freedom. We must be conscious that it is God's will that we should be free- that we should be good.

In all traditions of Christianity, obedience is considered as "the first of virtues." For monastics, in particular, perfect obedience, understood as "the mortification of the will" (cf. Phil. 2:8) is integral to all ascetic endeavour. Christian life would indeed be unthinkable without the basic notion of obedience. Alexander Schemamen is of the opinion that the Church Fathers do not speak of obedience in terms of normative requirements. Obedience transcends mere submissiveness with which it is commonly confused. The virtue of obedience occurs within the context of loving trust and personal relationship between two people in Christ, which *in itself* reveals the presence of Christ (cf. Mt. 18:20). Without this special relationship, one gains nothing from authority but pride, and nothing from obedience but guilt. Such feelings, however, defeat the very purpose of spiritual authority.

For Dr. Paulos Mar Gregorius it did not mean that human beings should remain obedient slaves, subject to command and authority; but that they should be grown up offspring, exercising authority.[10] Precisely speaking, authority is not the kind that exercises arbitrary dictatorship that we see in the functioning of a state. It is in the terms of freedom that God bestows upon every person. Terms and conditions formulated by state and organizations are meant to edify the citizens as good citizens, respecting the freedom- the promise of God- to attain divine. The misuse of authority has now been embedded in all spheres of life even in the church too. The bishop keeping in mind this notion-misuse of authority- in the state and church has expressed his views in his book "The Church and Authority."

The misuse of authority in the organized institutions caused erosion of the highly esteemed values that society has developed throughout centuries. Unfortunately, at present all churches are accused of misuse of authority. This, in fact, makes the topic very relevant. The notion of the misuse of authority may lead people to think that authority is bad in itself. In order to provide a better understanding of the purpose of authority in the church, Paulos Mar Gregorius made a special attempt to author a book called "The Church and Authority." In this paper I just concentrate on his effort to bring the notion of the charisma of authority in the churches into the consciousness of the leaders of churches. Today, compulsion, insistence and command are considered as means to exercise authority. This influences the church leaders and can cause division and disunity in different churches.

The functioning of the church is misconceived due to the influence of secularism. The churches are led astray regarding the original thrust of its existence. Hence there is need for rethinking on the nature of the church. Regarding this the author concludes with a very interesting statement which is noteworthy:

> Authority in the church is to be exercised in order that the Church can function as church; and what is the Church's function but the Worship of God and the Mission to the World? Authority is to be exercised in order that the Church may be truly edified, built up, in Christ by the Holy Spirit, that it may be enabled by the gift of the Spirit to fulfill its royal priesthood, as priests of the Nations before God and as Servant of God before the nations.[11]

According to the Bishop, authority is for *oikodome*, for worship and mission. He says that it is not an end in itself. Its purpose is not merely regulatory but also enabling. We worship God but we have to think as to what extent we are ready to witness the priesthood of Christ bestowed on every Christian in the world. Authority is the prospectus for a Christian to build the Church properly. Mission is not just a praxis for running institutions for the oppressed, the suppressed and the marginalized but an 'agent of enabling' our surroundings not only of human beings but of the entire creation to experience the living presence of the risen Christ. Authority cannot be confined within the framework of regulations, the tools for governance of a community but it is meant to build up that community in accordance with what it is to be.

Knowingly or unknowingly the concept of authority in the church becomes a point of contention. If there is any distinction envisaged in the hierarchy of the church that is merely functional and provisional, not essential. What is essential is the relationship of love and trust in Christ. Unity lived out even in diversity is precisely the promise of God to His Church. Any form or expression of authority, then must not be the expression of human pride but of humility before God, of assimilation to the divine hierarchy and of obedience to the will of Him who alone is called Father.[12]Such obedience is of the very essence not simply the well-being of humanity. Hierarchy exists in order to reveal the priestly vocation[13] and function of all within a world that is beautifully ordered by its Creator as cosmos.[14]

Authority in the Theological Pedagogy

In every organization for governance authority is essential. That is why hierarchy is structured in society. Theological training institutions also have the system of hierarchy that depicts authority. Relying upon the thoughts of the bishop one can articulate certain viewpoints that he envisaged regarding authority that has to be followed in theological training. As FFRRC, Kottayam celebrates its Ruby Year of existence, all of us, irrespective of teacher or student need to be aware of how to exercise authority in the church in general and in the seminaries. Many of us are serving our respective churches as pastors. The concept of Authority taught by Jesus Christ the Rabbi should be implemented in theological training, then only we can mould ourselves into good pastors. Only a good pastor can be a good theologian. Dr. Paulos Mar Gregorius upholds the Christ image as the theological tool to give orientation to the implementation of authority. He distinguishes between intrinsic authority and structural identity. Jesus taught with authority. This is what we see in the Scripture. If we interpret that Jesus was officially authorized by the structure of Jewish leaders as an expounder of the law of Moses, that would be a misinterpretation. He explained:

> .... Jesus had the source of authority in him, in his wisdom and power and love, in his integrity and holiness in the transparent truth of his words, in authentic ring of his personality. He said of course that all authority in heaven and on earth had been given to him by the Father, but what the people recognized was his own intrinsic authority, the authority of his personality and wisdom.[15]

The author proposed that "this kind of authority that church leaders should have." Unfortunately, today, this is what the church leadership lacks. Institutions and organizations inevitably require intrinsic authority and structural authority. Even in the church there are authority structures. Authority structures are all supposed to be conciliar in form, but in fact turn out to be authoritarian or bureaucratic.[16]He also made clear the consequences of this phenomenon: the breakdown of conciliar authority (i.e., of agape in community) goes hand in hand with the rise of authoritarian (monarchical), bureaucratic (commercial) or political (semblance of democracy) patterns.[17]Theological training, since it is an academic program, has its own methodology. Whatever it may be, if we fail in moulding our students to be 'Christ like', it is just a waste of time. One of the statements of Boris Bobrinskoy in this regard is very interesting:

> The Church is also humbled and brought down by the sins of its members. This is the Church's *kenosis*, or perhaps the *kenosis* of the Spirit whose radiance has been obscured.. ultimately, the Church's *kenosis* is a call to imitate the One who lowered himself – even washing his disciple's feet – and gave us an image of perfect humility. Humility and service, therefore, constitute an essential and inalienable aspect of the true exercise of authority in the Church.[18]

Dr. Paulos Mar Gregorius articulated a practical theology in this regard. He says:

> The ministry to which we are all called requires the whole of our being, the whole of our time, everything that we have. Only when everyone all over the world are prepared to lay down their whole lives, their precious time, their influence, their power, their wealth, their minds, their knowledge, their professions, all that they have, only then will

> the Church genuinely begin to bear fruit and fulfil the ministry, the glorious ministry to which Christ has called us.

He was very much aware of the fact that this ministry is not a bed of roses but rather a 'cross centered' one. He elucidates thus, "It is a ministry which may face failure and frustration, it is a ministry which will make us tired and torn, it is a ministry which will make us despised and rejected by all, knowing when we commit ourselves to him, who gave himself to us without reserve, then the glory, the hidden glory of the Lord, will begin to manifest itself in the world."

This is what the one who is engaged in theological training needs to keep in mind. The bishop is of the strong conviction that authority in the Church has to be structural as well as charismatic or intrinsic. The same concept is to be applied in theological pedagogy also. Anyone of these is neither superior nor inferior.

The Indian concept of teacher - student (Guru Sishya Bandham) relationship is noteworthy. One of the statements made by Swami Vinaya Chaitanya deserves special attention. He explained:

> Gurus are revaluators. They constantly restate the eternal truth to meet the requirements of the particular situation. Also, the disciple is greater than the Guru because he receives what is the Guru's and builds on it. He is the empty vessel that's filled. It is the disciple alone who has the Guru, who can understand the Guru. Thus s/he is greater than the Guru. Not greater in any social sense, but in the sense that the empty vessel is greater because of the possibility to be filled exists. And what is full can only be full of what is already filled with. [19]

Who is a real Guru? The answer is very obvious in the words of Swami Vinaya Chaitany as he expounds, "Guru is the one who is graphing proper prospectus for his disciples to be reborn to the pure ways of wisdom." [20]This sort of a Teacher (Great Guru), we experience in Jesus Christ. Christological analysis conducted by the bishop in this regard is very interesting to note here, he says,

"Jesus Christ did not bequeath to us any writings of his own; but He gave us the eucharist, wherein the heart of the Christian ministry is communicated to us."[21] He also deliberates that in the celebration of the eucharist in the church, we are not just commemorating the economy of salvation but in the Holy Spirit, we are all united with Christ and conformed to Christ.[22]Here is underlined the concept of being Christ like. He proposes that every Christian must grow into the image of 'Christ like' in the spheres of life.

Conclusion

This article is a humble attempt to put forward the concept of authority expounded by Dr. Paulos Mar Gregorius. Today this concept is highly misconceived by the society. Moreover, this influence is also upon the church leadership even in those engaged as teachers of theological training. This attitude is leading the church leaders to develop a counter witness. The Church, then, must be the reality where the dualism of authority and freedom is transcended through "obedience unto death" [23] and in love toward one another. If the issue of authority and obedience is to be examined creatively, we must first, clarify our understanding about how we, as Church, can become a more loving and serving community. Obedience is a mystery revealed by the Holy Spirit and experienced as sacrament in the life of the Church. Present realities and structures will continue to exist. Yet we must learn to be more open, allowing the Spirit to be more active in us. During his ministry, Christ was asked on several occasions by what authority he acted. In fact, he never explicitly answered this question. Rather, he responded by the way he lived, that is by the authority of love incarnate. Authority outside this Christ-like love is an arbitrary tyranny. Authority lived in the laying down of life for one's neighbor[24], on the other hand, is creative and life-giving. May the picture of our Lord Jesus Christ as He washes the feet of his disciples be an inspiration to continue to make the teaching ministry of FFRRC a unique one.

{Fr. Dr. Ninan K. George, an ordained priest of the Malankara Orthodox Syrian Church, serving as a Professor and Research Guide in the department of Christian Theology at the Orthodox Theological Seminary and the Federated Faculty for Research in Religion and Culture, (FFRRC) Kottayam. He authored many books and articles.}

Endnotes

[1] Gregorios, Paulos, *The Church and Authority*, 32.

[2] Gregorios, Paulos, *The Church and Authority*, 32.

[3] Gregorios, Paulos, *The Church and Authority*, 32.

[4] Gregorios, Paulos, *The Church and Authority*, 33.

[5] Gregorios, Paulos, *The Church and Authority*, 33.

[6] See Romans 13: 1

[7] Gregorios, Paulos, *The Church and Authority*, 34.

[8] Gregorios, Paulos, *The Church and Authority*, 34.

[9] Gregorios, Paulos, *The Church and Authority*, 34.

[10] Gregorios, Paulos, *The Church and Authority*, 35.

[11] Gregorios, Paulos Mar. *The Church and Authority*, 36.

[12] Cf. Mathew 23.9.

[13] Cf. 1 Peter 2.9.

[14] Schmemann, Alexander. *Church World Mission*, 186.

[15] Gregorios, Paulos, *The Church and Authority*, 42.

[16] Gregorios, Paulos, *The Church and Authority*, 42.

[17] Gregorios, Paulos. *The Church and Authority*, 42.

[18] Bobrinskoy, Boris. *The Mystery of the Church*, 17.

[19] Chaitanya, Swami Vinaya, In Honour of Guruhood. *A Vision of Beauty*, 311.

[20] Cf. Chaitanya, Swami Vinaya. In Honour of Guruhood, *A Vision of Beauty*, 311.

[21] Gregoros, Paulos. *The Kingdom of Diakonia*, 84.

[22] See Gregorios, Paulos. *The Kingdom of Diakonia*, 85.

[23] Cf. Philippians 2:8.

[24] Cf. John 10:11.

■■■

Contemporary Trinitarian Readings of Pluralism: Commitment and Openness

Rev. Dr. John Philip A.

Introduction

Faith cannot be divorced from living realities. Hence Christian theology cannot exclude contemporary realities from its theological enterprises. Therefore, theology should take place within a cultural and linguistic context.[1] Fresh theology is made up of new possibilities and emerging challenges.[2] We are living in the midst of intense pluralism. Contemporary pluralistic society faces the trauma of uncertainty and the threat of the survival of creation. This paper attempts to reread the contemporary trinitarian understanding for a pluralistic society endangered by the COVID -19 pandemic.

The doctrine of the Trinity has emerged as a significant Christian doctrine in our era after many years of its being ignored. With its resurgence, it has been interpreted in terms of society, liberation, ecology, feminism, etc. A good number of theologians have tried to develop a theology of religious pluralism in relation with trinitarian understanding.[3] Jacques Dupuis opines, "The datum of faith and the living context of religious pluralism must be brought together."[4]Therefore, the doctrine of the Trinity is not only a way of understanding God and Christ but also fundamentally a conception of life.[5]

Contemporary Discussion on Trinitarian Theology of Religious Pluralism

Trinitarian understanding has recently been presented as an effective framework for working out a coherent theology of religions in the contemporary discussion on a Christian theology of religious pluralism.

Jacques Dupuis attempted to formulate a Christian theology of religious pluralism by interpreting the doctrine of the Trinity. According to him, "The doctrine of the triune God does not merely stand at the centre of the Christian message and doctrine; it also imprints a Trinitarian rhythm on the *exodus* of all things from God and their *eisodos* toward God."[6] Dupuis offers a new approach to the theology of religions in which the work of the Spirit of the triune God in other religions may be viewed as distinctive and even different from God's Word in Jesus but yet not contradictory to that Word.[7] For him, religious pluralism is more than a matter of fact because it is grounded in the superabundant riches and variety of God's self-manifestations to humanity.

Gavin D'Costa is sure that the trinitarian understanding makes possible a genuine Christian response to world religions because it takes the particularities of history entirely and seriously.[8] He proposes five theses from the trinitarian understanding for a Christian understanding. The Trinitarian Christology guards against exclusivism and pluralism by dialectically relating the universal and the particular. Pneumatology allows the particularity of Christ to be related to the universal activity of God in the history of humankind. Christocentric trinitarianism discloses a loving relationship as the proper mode of being which helps one to love people of other religions as neighbours. The normativity of Christ involves the normativity of crucified self-giving love, praxis and dialogue. The church stands under the judgment of the Holy Spirit, and if the Holy Spirit is active in the world religions, then the world religions are vital to Christian faithfulness.[9] The doctrine of the Trinity stipulates against an exclusive identification of God and Jesus, as well as against a non-identification of God and Jesus.[10]For him, Christian pluralism is a species of enlightenment modernity.[11] D'Costa sees the pluralistic goals of openness, tolerance and equality in trinitarian theology.[12]

Unlike Paul F. Knitter, D'Costa connects the Spirit's presence in other religions to Christ. Unlike Raimundo Panikkar, he does not relativise Christ as only one reference point and unlike Dupuis, he connects the Spirit's presence with the Church and kingdom.[13] The same Spirit helps the church to follow the Christ present in other religions. He is at once loyal to the Church and other religions. But D'Costa neglects the divine mystery which is surely a meeting point for religions.

Mark Heim also affirms the trinitarian plurality as the ground of religious plurality. Like the variety of relations within God, there is "the possibility of a variety of distinct relations with God." Mark Heim suggests a new proposal regarding the religious ends from the perspective of trinitarian understanding.[14] For him, different religions pursue different goals.[15] Though it helps to appreciate the particular dimension of a religion, he divides religions both in respect of path and goal.

Raimundo Panikkar distinguishes three spiritualities in Trinity, namely, 'iconolatry' or path of the karma of ritual, 'personalism' or path of loving devotion, and 'mysticism', a path of unitive knowledge in different religions. For him, all these three spiritualities are to be found in the doctrine of the Trinity.[16] The threefold traces of the Trinity extend their arena not only to world religions but also to every reality.[17] Thus he proposes trinitarian plurality in a very general context.

According to Raimundo Panikkar, "pluralism penetrates into the very heart of the ultimate reality."[18] He sees the scope of trinitarian theology in its universal dimension. Panikkar explicitly denies that there can be an ultimate reduction of the phenomenal plurality into an all-encompassing new systematization and asserts that the incommensurability of ultimate systems is unbridgeable.

S. J. Samartha stands for the trinitarian mystery which acknowledges the limitation of the response. The incomprehensibility of God highlighted by Samartha is the very basis of the trinitarian doctrine. This is the reason for various responses and thus different religions. For him, the Hindu doctrine of Brahman and the Christian doctrine of the Trinity are two responses to the one transcendent mystery that lies beyond Hinduism and Christianity. Both responses are the result of different historical and cultural conditions.

The doctrine of the Trinity, for Samartha, is only a symbol and therefore cannot adequately describe the inner ontological working of mystery, but can only point to the mystery.[19] According to Samartha, any particular religious response to mystery cannot be separated as superior, unique, or normative for the rest.[20] He sees the unity of all religions in a transcendent mystery that lies beyond all religions. But Samartha fails to give attention to the trinitarian relationality and hence the uniqueness of the trinitarian understanding.

Though he could not develop a trinitarian theology of religions, his basic assumptions matched with certain aspects of the trinitarian theology. For him, the absolute finality of Jesus Christ faces the danger of Christomonism. It is a fact that the trinitarian doctrine transcends Christomonism, but Jesus Christ is the distinctive particularity of the Christian faith.

According to Clark Pinnock, the challenge of pluralism is not new and it makes problems for the contemporary human due to the "relativistic mindset of late modernity."[21] He introduces an alternative trinitarian understanding. Pinnock explains the divine presence and work in the world through his trinitarian understanding of God. He sees the trinitarian love incarnated in Jesus Christ and experienced through participation in the Holy Spirit.[22]For him, "Christ, the only mediator, sustains particularity, while the Spirit, the presence of God everywhere safeguards universality."[23] He believes that revelation is universal because the Spirit is everywhere at work. The Spirit "can foster transforming friendship with God anywhere and everywhere."[24] The ministries of the Son and the Spirit cannot be put in any kind of opposition to one another. This ontology points to the relationality and openness in the nature of God. His inclusivism is grounded in a relational ontology in the being of the triune God.

The cross is the centre of Moltmann's trinitarian theology.[25] He stands for a sincere dialogue among religions "out of the depths of the understanding of God."[26] The depth is in the cross of Jesus Christ. His respect for the otherness rests neither on mere tolerance nor on an abstract dialectic of identity and difference, nor on speculation about the unity and diversity in the triune life, but on the triune God's openness and the radical otherness expressed in the life of Jesus.[27]

Moltmann's pneumatology accepts the free activity and manifold gifts of the Holy Spirit. He wants the Church to free itself from the idea of undialectical priority of the Son to the Spirit. The Spirit opens the eternal life of the triune God to the world. For this understanding, Moltmann depends much on the

Cappadocian Fathers. The plurality of the religions, for him is not because of original sin or revelation but by the multiplicity of the gifts of the Spirit.[28] If the religions serve the Spirit of life, it is due to the presence of the Spirit. He wants to place the question of the relationship of Christianity and the other religions in a strong trinitarian, Christological, and pneumatological context.[29]

Amos Yong inquires how it is possible to harmonise the affirmation of the universal divine presence with the particularity of Jesus Christ.[30] The Christology and pneumatology must be understood within a broader trinitarian framework. Yong envisages a trinitarian theology in which there is a mutual relationship between the economy of the Son and the Spirit.

For Amos Yong, discerning the presence and activity of the Spirit in the religions is central to a theology of religions. He follows the criteria for discernment proposed by Hans Küng, which are a general ethical criteria: faithfulness to canonical origins and the specifically Christian criterion of Christ.[31] It is a fact that these criteria may be contradicted sometimes.

From the above survey of theologians, it is a fact that the trinitarian understanding has become a source for Christian theology of religious pluralism. While Raimundo Panikkar, S. J. Samartha, and Jacques Dupuis see an ontological basis for pluralism in the doctrine of the Trinity, Gavin D'Costa and Clark Pinnock use the trinitarian understanding with much reservation.

Trinitarian Theology as a Model of Mutuality, Relationality, and Diversity

The formula 'one *ousia* three *hypostases*' clarified the unity and distinction in the doctrine of the Trinity. The *ousia* is common and the *hypostases* are distinctive. Both oneness and diversity rest in the Trinity. Leonardo Boff points out, "In our experience of the

Mystery there is indeed diversity (Father, Son and Holy Spirit) and at the same time unity in this diversity, through the communion of the different Persons by which each is in the others, with the others, through the others and for the others."[32]The three divine Persons have something in common that enables them to relate to each other, enhance each other and achieve ever greater unity among themselves. Commonality and diversity are ontological reality in the triune God.

As God is the source of life, unity and plurality are the Reality of all realities. According to Colin E. Gunton, "The plurality in unity of the triune revelation enables us to do justice to the diversity, richness, and openness of the world without denying its unity in relativist versions of pluralism."[33] The unity and plurality are essential bi-polarities of a Christian theology of pluralism. Though the religions and ideologies are distinctive, there are commonalities among them. The commonalities help them to transcend their differences without doing away with them.[34]It is not only one nature of the Trinity variously and inadequately expressed by different religious traditions but also the plurality of religions as a reality of the one Godhead. The diversity is, therefore, one aspect of the process of the history. The other aspect is unity, and the two complement each other in the continuous process of self-unification in self-differentiation.[35]

Diversity as Theological Reality

The Father is unique, the Son is unique, and the Holy Spirit is unique in their special properties. The uniqueness of each divine hypostasis grounds the distinction of the persons.[36]Michael Jinkins rightly points out the theological implication of the diversity. For him, "Diversity is not primarily a sociological and historical phenomenon, but a theological reality with profound sociological and historical implications."[37]Tom F. Driver observes, "It is that there are real and genuine differences within the Godhead itself, owing to the manifold involvements that God has undertaken with the great variety of human communities."[38]The trinitarian theology approves both respect for the other and completes this otherness as pure neighbourly difference.[39]

Relationality and 'Other'

The deepest expression of personhood is unconditional love. The Father, the Son and the Spirit are united together in perfect love.[40]The love in freedom is the self-expression of His /Her very being.[41] The divine love is the source of relationality to others. The trinitarian relationality offers possibilities for drawing analogies between the being of God and that of the world.[42] Relationality and otherness constitute the two-sided dialectic.[43] The doctrine of the Trinity offers a clue to address the 'Other' as a distinctive identity and mutual indwelling of the 'Others'. The well-being of the 'Other' is constitutive of the identity of God.[44]

The relationality of the Trinity actualises in history. History and its particular events find meaning in the trinitarian relationality. The 'Other' is constitutive of the core of ultimate reality. It is helpful to know one's own faith more deeply.[45] Pluralism is the one area in which distinctiveness and the mutuality should co-exist. Panikkar underlines, "Each religion may be a dimension of the other in a kind of Trinitarian *perichorēsis* or *circumincessio*."[46] The interpenetration of the living realities promotes both mutual correction and mutual enrichment.[47] Pluralistic resources can be greatly enriching one another.

The Trinity as a community of mutual indwelling shows a paradigm for the human community. The mutual love of the Trinity can be shown in community.[48]The eternal mutual self-giving-in-love of the trinitarian Persons provides us with the ontology of love to replace the ontology of violence.[49] Hence, Christians are called to reflect this loving communion in their communion with others.[50]

As the Holy Spirit perfects every operation of the Trinity, the Spirit facilitates human participation in God's inner love.[51] The overflowing love of the Trinity allows space for the existence of all creative actions. Hence, the Divine love provides fellowship, equality of opportunity and generosity.[52] As religion is the one area of human creativity, it has the possibility of expressing the divine love. Religious pluralism, for Jacques Dupuis, "belongs to the nature of the overflowing communication of the triune God."[53]The divine love provides space for all realities and speaks in many ways. This overflowing love is the basis for plurality.

Overcoming Religious Fundamentalism

Gregory of Nazianzus does not follow the literal interpretation of the Scripture. The literal interpretation ends in fundamentalism.[54] Gregory seeks the "hidden inner meanings' of the text.[55] The limitation of the language pointed out by Gregory is surely helpful in avoiding bibliolatry. It is agreed that the Scripture reaches humans in a human language set in time. It in no way alters faith in its truth.[56] A fundamentalist use of the Bible negates the message of pluralism and tolerance.[57]

The literal interpretation of the Scripture leads to religious fundamentalism.[58] One of the basic characteristics of fundamentalism is affirming the superiority of one religion over other religions.[59] It believes that God is specially interested only in the adherents of that particular religion or religious school, and would exclude others from the inner circle of the privileged. It is usually exclusivist and polemic in its temper.

The consequence of a fundamentalist attitude is religious arrogance which creates violence. Christian fundamentalism exercises violence at various levels: It does violence to the Bible, humans and their gift of reason, free will, the variety of life-plans, and thus individual ways to relate to God.[60] According to Paulos Mar Gregorios, "Religious fundamentalism is politically and economically conservative or reactionary, anti-progressive, anti-rational, anti-socialist."[61]

Religions have a role in fostering values and norms.[62] In this way they can be channels of life, which are able to build civilisations.[63] But fundamentalism creates tension in the community, which in turn bifurcates society. By affirming the incomprehensibility of God and the limitation of religious language, one can transcend religious fundamentalism. Every conception is inadequate. It means that either no one knows what the divine actually is or it allows saying of the divinity in a number of ways.[64]

Universal Presence of the Trinitarian God

Leonardo Boff says, "Creation is of the Trinity, comes from the Trinity, goes to the Trinity; reflects the Trinity, but is not the Trinity."[65] As the humanity is entrusted with the divine creativity, the human enterprises are of the Trinity.[66]The Creator is revealed in and through the creation. So, the world reveals the being of God by virtue of its capacity to be a framework for culture. This inadequate knowledge is the source of immense differences in the tradition.

Kevin J. Vanhoozer contends that if the Holy Spirit's activity is universal, how can the divine be distinguished from the demonic?[67] It is through the discerning power of the Holy Spirit. The Holy Spirit in a community allows the discernment of the fruit of the Holy Spirit in the community. The socio-historical life of religions as such cannot be taken as the work of the Holy Spirit.[68]

The universality of God's agency and presence has to be taken seriously as the theological basis for an adequate Christian understanding of the religions. Therefore, the doctrine of the Trinity on creation provides the narrative space for human endeavours including the religions. Christoph Schwöbel affirms, "No part of reality can be excluded from the sphere of God's activity and presence and every form of knowledge relies on God as the ground of its possibility and as the source of its truth."[69]Each religion needs to be attentive to other religions. It helps to enrich one's own self-understanding.

Trinitarian Theology for a Christian Theology of Pluralism

It is a fact that rigid monotheism intensifies exclusivism.[70]The monotheistic religions, in general, are more intolerant to and suppressive of pluralism. Walter Brueggemann considers, "Monotheism is problematic as a social practice because it invites all kinds of reductionisms that are undertaken to be equated with or commensurate with, or in any case inevitably derived from Yahweh's singleness."[71] It tempts to equate one God with one religion. It assumes that the monotheistic God wants only one religion to be practised by all humans. This results in exclusive claims.[72]

Leonardo Boff notes, "Strict monotheism can justify totalitarianism and the concentration of power in one person's hands, in politics and in religion."[73] The sole divine power without any sharing in the Godhead is endorsed power-accumulation to human systems. In rigid monotheism, pluralism is seen as an imperfection to be overcome because God is one and the same. M. Von Brück opinions, "Such an understanding of God does promote doctrinal intolerance and social hegemonic attitudes. The result may well be totalitarianism in all its different forms."[74] In this context, trinitarian theology is helpful to formulate a Christian theology of pluralism.

Commitment and Openness

The trinitarian orientation meets the demands for openness, tolerance, and equality.[75]Openness is not an uncritical acceptance of all things in history. It makes sure of the commitment to one's own religion and at the same time openness to other religions.[76] So, the rinitarian theology acknowledges particularities of different religions seriously and provides space for conversation with other particularities. Commitment and openness should go hand in hand.

Theocentric theologians give too little attention to the significance of history and the important contribution the person of Jesus makes to history. Attention is given to the presence of God in other religions.[77]Christocentric theologians exalt the person of Jesus in order to neglect the divine presence in other world religions. But trinitarian theology intertwines both theocentrism and Christocentrism. The commitment to Jesus of Christocentrism and the openness of theocentrism can go hand in hand in trinitarian theology.

The pluralistic inclusivism approves mutual interaction and transformation.[78] This is approved by trinitarian theology. But the trinitarian relationality has not merged the particularities. John B. Cobb retains the idea of mutual transformation and the particularity of each religion.[79] The trinitarian relationality finds its fullness in divine mystery. Though the trinity is relational, the human cannot say what the divine mystery ultimately is. But the divine mystery for a Christian theology of religious pluralism is not developed by Cobb. The trinitarian theology of religious pluralism integrates both divine mystery and relationality-in-diversity.

Critical and Creative Interactions of the Living Realities

The trinitarian theology not only affirms the religious pluralism but also transforms religions as part of the divine intervention in creation. Along with appreciating the goodness of the religions they have to engage in critical interaction. Tom F. Driver comments, "Variety is not only the 'spice' of life: without it, evil is more likely to go unchecked, potential for good more apt to perish unrealized."[80] The Christian theology aims to reveal the forms of violence that structure society.[81] The trinitarian approach rests in discerning religions including Christianity. It upholds both the goodness of religious pluralism and the abolition of the status-quo maintaining of the pluralistic approach.

The early Christians saw in history traces of angelic and demonic powers.[82]The Christian theology of religious pluralism puts forward the particularity of Jesus Christ to critically evaluate religious values.[83] Jesus Christ is the criterion to discern history.[84] Hence, Christian theology presents the liberating mission of the crucified and risen Lord who is to be found among the disenfranchised of society without excluding any other particularity.[85] So one's own criteria cannot be abandoned at any stage. The basis of one's faith commitment is a necessity. One can accept other criteria later in conversation with his own criteria. In that process he/she may find the limitation of one's own given criteria.

A Christian theology of pluralism aims at the dialogical coexistence of the communities in the community. This is a change away from their introverted and self-centred existence towards dialogical pro-existence.[86] In order to have creative existence, people of different faiths and no faiths need dialogue at the level of both theory and praxis. Religions are not only complementary they are rather supplementary. They support and enforce one another.[87] They help to achieve common commitment to an action for a better society.[88]

Conclusion

Plurality in the Godhead is a sure sign of plurality within other God-given realities. It is not to be suppressed, but to be affirmed based on divine plurality. Plurality is not an end in itself. There is a unity beyond plurality. The unity is not in losing one's own identity, but it also involves mutual indwelling and is enriching. The mutual indwelling of the triune Persons is the overflowing of divine love. The trinitarian love penetrates over creation in manifold ways to enhance divine love. The relationality-diversity pendulum of trinitarian theology balances the two poles of interpenetration and distinctiveness. These two are necessary components of a theology of pluralism.

The trinitarian understanding promotes unity rather than division, and love rather than hate. Survival of the created order, particularly that of the humans, rests upon the mutual relationship among different communities. In order to heal the world, the true friendship and relationality, derived from the genuine love of the triune God, which was revealed in Jesus Christ and universally present in and through the Holy Spirit, are required. Thus, the reconciliation of the fragmented world is possible through acknowledging plurality and coming together of communities.

{Rev. Dr. John Philip A. is the former Principal of Mar Thoma Episcopal Jubilee Institute of Evangelism, Kombady and the former Director of TMAM Research and Orientation Centre, Manganam. Currently he serves as the Professor and research guide in the department of Christian theology in Mar Thoma Theological Seminary and FFRRC, Kottayam.}

Endnotes

[1] Gordon D. Kaufman, *The Theological Imagination* (Philadelphia: The Westminster, 1981), 23.

[2] Cf. M. Thomas Thangaraj, "Teaching Theology in a Multifaith Context: A New Approach to Teaching Systematic Theology," in *Ministerial Formation in a Multi-faith Milieu*, edited by Sam Amritham and S. Wesley Ariarajah (Geneva: WCC, 1985), 29.

[3] Raimundo Panikkar sees the mystery of the Trinity as the ultimate foundation for pluralism;("The Jordan, the Tiber, and the Ganges: Three Kairological Moments of Christic Self-Consciousness," in *The Myth of Christian Uniqueness Toward a Pluralistic Theology of Religions*, 110). For S. J. Samartha, the Trinitarian mystery provides the ontological basis for tolerance (*One Christ Many Religions*, 94-95). Gavin D'Costa wants to give a trinitarian framework to religious pluralism: "If the Holy Spirit is active in the world religions, then the world religions are vital to Christian faithfulness" ("Christ, the Trinity, and Religious Plurality," in *Christian Uniqueness Reconsidered: The Myth of a Pluralistic Theology of Religions*, 23). S. Mark Heim draws out the possibility of many salvations from the Christian doctrine of the Trinity (S. Mark Heim, *The Depth of Riches: A Trinitarian Theology of Religious Ends*, 219; Stanley J. Grenz, "Toward an Evangelical Theology of the Religions," *JES* 31/2 (1994): 49-65; Veli-Matti Kärkkäinen, *Trinity and Religious Pluralism* (Burlington: Ashgate, 2004); Kevin J. Vanhoozer, *The Trinity in a Pluralistic Age: Theological Essays on Culture and Religion* (Grand Rapids, Michigan: The Eerdmans Publishing Company, 1997)).

[4] Jacques Dupuis, *Toward a Christian Theology of Religious Pluralism* (Indian Edition, Anand: Gujarat Sahitya Prakash, 2001), 16. See Christoph Schwöbel, "Plurality, Universality, and the Religions, in *Christian Uniqueness Reconsidered The Myth of a Pluralistic Theology of Religions*, 34.

[5] See Boris Bobrinskoy, *The Mystery of the Trinity: Trinitarian Experience and Vision in the Biblical and Patristic Tradition* (Crestwood, New York: St. Vladimir's Seminary Press, 1999), 4.

[6] Jacques Dupuis, *Toward a Christian Theology of Religious Pluralism*, 262. Jacques Dupuis is the most influential and controversial Catholic theologian in the field of theology of religions.

[7] Daniel L. Migliore, "The Trinity and the Theology of Religions," in *God's Life in Trinity*, edited by Miroslav Volf and Michael Welker (Minneapolis: Fortress Press, 2006), 102.

[8] Gavin D'Costa, "Christ, the Trinity and Religious Plurality," in *Christian Uniqueness Reconsidered* (Maryknoll, New York: Orbis Books, 1992), 17.

[9] *Ibid.*, 18-25.

[10] Gavin D'Costa, "An Examination of the Pluralist Paradigm in the Christian Theology of Religions," *Scottish Journal of Theology* 39 (1968): 211-224.

[11] Gavin D'Costa, *The Meeting of Religions and the Trinity* (Maryknoll, New York: Orbis Books, 2000), 1-2.

[12] *Ibid.*, 99.

[13] Veli-Matti Kärkkäinen, *An Introduction to the Theology of Religions* (Downers Grove, Illinois: InterVarsity Press, 2003), 222.

[14] S. Mark Heim, *The Depth of the Riches: A Trinitarian Theology of Religious EndsReligion*, 219.

[15] S. Mark Heim, *Salvations: Truth and Difference inReligions* (Maryknoll, New York: Orbis Books, 1995), 225-226.

[16] Raimundo Panikkar, *Trinity and the Religious Experience of Man* (Maryknoll, New York: Orbis Books, 1973), 42.

[17] *Ibid.*, xiv.

[18] Raimundo Panikkar, "Religious Pluralism: The Metaphysical Challenge," in *Religious Pluralism*, in Boston University Studies in Philosophy and Religion, volume 5, edited by Leroy S. Rouner (Notre Dame: University of Notre Dame Press, 1984), 110.

[19] Stanley J. Samartha, "The Cross and the Rainbow Christ in a Multireligious Culture," in *The Myth of Christian Uniqueness Toward a Pluralistic Theology of Religions*,edited by John Hick and Paul Knitter (Maryknoll, New York, Orbis Books, 1987), 76.

[20] James L. Fredericks, *Faith among Faiths* (New York: Paulist Press, 1999), 13.

[21] Clark Pinnock, *A Wideness in God's Mercy: The Finality of Jesus Christ in a World of Religions* (Grand Rapids, Michigan: Wm. B. Eerdmans Publishing Company, 1992), 9.

[22] Clark Pinnock, "An Inclusivist View," in *More Than One Way? Four Views on Salvation in a Pluralistic World.*, 103.

[23] Clark Pinnock, *Flame of Love: A Theology of the Holy Spirit* (Illinois: Intervarsity Press, 1996), 192.

[24] *Ibid.*, 187.

[25] Jürgen Moltmann, "Is 'Pluralist Theology' Useful for the Dialogue of World Religions?" in *ChristianUniqueness Reconsidered*, 152.

[26] Jürgen Moltmann, *The Church in the Power of the Holy Spirit* (New York: Harper & Row, 1977), 161.

[27] Daniel L. Migliore, "The Trinity and the Theology of Religions," in *God's Life in Trinity*, edited by Miroslav Volf and Michael Welker (Minneapolis: Fortress Press, 2006), 109.

[28] Jürgen Moltmann, Nocholas Wolterstorff and Ellen T. Charry, *A Passion for God's Reign* (Grand Rapids, Michigan: The Eerdmans Publishing Company, 1998), 62.

[29] Daniel L. Migliore, "The Trinity and the Theology of Religions," in *God's Life in Trinity*, 113.

[30] Amos Yong, *Discerning the Spirit(s): A Pentecostal-Charismatic Contribution to Christian Theology of Religions* (Sheffield: Sheffield Academic Press, 2000), 35.

[31] *Ibid.*, 141. See Hans Küng, "What Is True Religion? Toward an Ecumenical Christology," in Toward a Universal Theology of Religion, edited by Leonard Swidler (Maryknoll, New York: Orbis Books, 1988), 231-250.

[32] Leonardo Boff, *Trinity and Society*(Maryknoll, New York, Orbis Books, 1988), 3.

[33] Colin Gunton, "The Trinity, natural Theology, and a Theology of nature," in The *Trinity in a Pluralistic Age Theological Essays on Culture and Religion*, 103. Cf. Rowan D. Williams, "Trinity and Pluralism," in *Christian Uniqueness Reconsidered The Myth of a Pluralistic Theology of Religions*, 4.

[34] Jacques Dupuis, *Toward a Christian Theology of Religious Pluralism*, 232.

[35] M. Von Brück, "Religious Pluralism and Our Understanding of God," *Indian Theological Studies* 26/1 (March 1989): 45.

[36] Gregory, "Against Eunomius" II, 2, in *Nicene and Post Nicene Fathers* 5, 10.

[37] Michael Jinkins, "Mutuality and Difference: trinity, creation and the theological ground of the church's unity," *Scottish Journal of Theology* 56/2 (2003): 149.

[38] Tom F. Driver, "The Case for Pluralism," in *The Myth of Christian Uniqueness Toward a Pluralistic Theology of Religions*, 212.

[39] John Milbank, "End of Dialogue," 188.

[40] Leonardo Boff, *Trinity and Society*,54.

[41] M. Von Brück, "Religious Pluralism and Our Understanding of God," in *Indian Theological Studies* 26/1 (March 1989): 45.

[42] Colin Gunton, "The Trinity, Natural Theology, and a Theology of nature," in *The Trinity in a Pluralistic Age Theological Essays on Culture and Religion*, 103.

[43] Jürgen Moltmann, *The Spirit of Life: A Universal Affirmation* (London: SCM, 1992), 103.

[44] *Ibid.*, 10-14, 47-51, 58-77, 114-22.

[45] Kevin J. Vanhoozer, "Does the Trinity Belong in a Theology of Religions?" *The Trinity in a Pluralistic Age: Theological Essays on Culture and Religion*, 67.

[46] Michael Ipgrave, *Trinity and Inter-Faith Dialogue Plentitude and Plurality*, 11.

[47] Raimundo Panikkar, "The Jordan, the Tiber, and the Ganges: Three Kairological Moments of Christic Self-Consciousness," in *The Myth of Christian Uniqueness Toward a Pluralistic Theology of Religions*, 112.

[48] John B. Cobb introduces the idea of mutual transformation in an internal level. He affirms the possibility to have mutual transformation of Christianity and Mahāyāna Buddhism. See John B. Cobb, *Beyond Dialogue Toward a Mutual Transformation of Christianity and Buddhism* (Philadelphia: Fortress Press, 1982), 52.

[49] Stanley Grenz and John R. Franke, *Beyond Foundationism Shaping Theology*

in a Postmodern Context (Lousville, Kentucky: John Knox Press,2001), 201.

[50] Lesslie Newbigin, "The Trinity as Public Truth," *The Trinity in a Pluralistic Age Theological Essays on Culture and Religion*, 6.

[51] Gavin D'Costa, "Christ, the Trinity and Religious Plurality," in *Christian Uniqueness Reconsidered The Myth of a Pluralistic Theology of Religions*, 19-20.

[52] Gavin D'Costa, *The Meeting of Religions and the Trinity*, 121.

[53] Leonardo Boff, *Trinity and Society*, 151.

[54] Jacques Dupuis, *Toward a Christian Theology of Religious Pluralism*, Indian Edition, 387. Cf. Jacques Dupuis, *Christianity and the Religions*, 263.

[55] The only possible faith was one emerged from a literal interpretation of the Scripture. They identified it as the sole, supreme, inerrant conveyor of divine truth. They have absolute claims and express intolerance to other religions. See Brenda E. Brasher, "Introduction," *Encyclopedia of Fundamentalism*, edited by Brenda E. Brasher (New York: Routledge, 2001): xv.

[56] Gregory, "Against Eunomius" III. 2, in *NPNF* 5, 137-138.

[57] Cf. Stuart E. Brown, trans., *The Challenge of the Scriptures*, in *Faith Meets Faith Series*, edited by Paul F. Knitter (Maryknoll, New York: Orbis Books, 1989), 87.

[58] Alexander M. Schweitzer, "Fundamentalism-A Challenge for the Catholic Biblical Federation," in *Biblical Apostolate and Religious Fundamentalism*, edited by A Peter Abir (Chennai: Catholic Biblical Federation, 2004), 34-35.

[59] The term 'fundamentalism', introduced in *Watchman-Examiner*, an American Baptist magazine, was derived from *the Fundamentals* which referred to a set of tracts from earlier in the century. Oxford Dictionary defines fundamentalism as "strict maintenance of traditional orthodox religious beliefs such as the fundamentals of the Protestant Christianity."

[60] Scaria Thuruthiyil, "The Phenomenon of Religious Fundamentalism," in *Dialogical Dynamics of Religions*, ed. Augustine Thottakara (Bangalore: Dharmaram Publications, 1993), 47.

[61] Alexander M. Schweitzer, "Fundamentalism-A Challenge for the Catholic Biblical Federation," in *Biblical Apostolate and Religious Fundamentalism*, 34.

[62] Paulos Mar Gregorios, *The Secular Ideology: An Impotent Remedy for India's Communal Problem* (Delhi: ISPCK, 1998), 67.

[63] Cf. A. Nunuk P. Murniati, "The Role of Religion in Fostering Life," in *Springs of Living Water*, edited by Marlene Perera and A. Nunuk P. Murniati (Bangalore: The Ecumenical Association of Third World Theologians, 1997), 55.

[64] Cf. Hendrik Vroom, *No Other Gods* (Grand Rapids, Michigan: Wm. B. Eerdmans Publishing Company, 1983), viii.

[65] *Ibid.*, 45.

[66] Leonardo Boff, *Trinity and Society*, 221.

[67] Colin Gunton, "The Trinity,Nnatural Theology, and a Theology of nature," in *The Trinity in a Pluralistic Age Theological Essays on Culture and Religion*, 98.

[68] Kevin J. Vanhoozer, "Does the Trinity Belong in a Theology of Religions?" in *The Trinity in a Pluralistic Age Theological Essays on Culture and Religion*, 63. See Gavin D'Costa, *Theology and Religious Pluralism: The Challenge of Other Religions* (Oxford: Blackwell, 1986), 135.

[69] Gavin D'Costa, *The Meeting of Religions and the Trinity*, 128.

[70] Christoph Schwöbel, "Plurality, Universality, and the Religions, in Gavin D'Costa, *Christian Uniqueness Reconsidered: The Myth of a Pluralistic Theology of Religions*, 38.

[71] Paul Tillich, *Christianity and the Encounter of the World Religions* (New York: Columbia Press, 1963), 31.

[72] Walter Brueggemann, "Exodus in the Plural (Amos 9:7)," in *Many Voices One God: Being Faithful in a Pluralistic Context* (Louisville, Kentucky: John Knox Press, 1998), 19.

[73] Rita M. Gross, "Religious Diversity: Some implication for Monotheism," *Cross Currents* 49/3 (Fall 1993), 354.

[74] Leonardo Boff, *Trinity and Society*, 20.

[75] Brück M. Von, "Religious Pluralism and Our Understanding of God," in *Indian Theological Studies* 26/1 (March 1989): 39.

[76] Gavin D'Costa, *The Meeting of Religions and the Trinity*, 99.

[77] John B. Cobb affirms, "In faithfulness to Christ I must be open to others." See "The Meaning of Pluralism for Christian Self-Understanding," in *Religious Pluralism* (Notre Dame: University of Notre Dame Press, 1984), 174.

[78] Ian Kerr, "Incarnation, Mission and Religious Pluralism," *Trinity Occasional Papers* XIII/1 (July 1994): 35-36.

[79] K. P. Aleaz, *Theology of Religions* (Calcutta: Momita Publishers, 1998), 192.

[80]John B. Cobb, Jr, in his book *Beyond Dialogue: Toward a Mutual Transformation of Christianity and Buddhism*, has attempted to show how Christianity and Mahāyāna Buddhism can transform one another without losing the particularities.

[81] Tom F. Driver, "The Case for Pluralism," in *The Myth of Christian Uniqueness Toward a Pluralistic Theology of Religions*, 213.

[82] Gavin D'Costa, *The Meeting of Religions and the Trinity*, 123.

[83] Paul Tillich, *Christianity and the Encounter of the World Religions*, 85.

[84] *Ibid*., 82.

[85] *Ibid*., 81.

[86] Orlando E. Costas, "A Radical Evangelical Contribution from Latin America," in *Christ's Lordship and Religious Pluralism*, 154.

[87] S. Arokiasamy, "Theology of Religions from Liberation Perspective," in *Religious Pluralism*, 300.

[88] Dominic Veliath, "Jesus Christ and the Theology of Religions: A Conspectus of Models," in *Religious Pluralism*, 169.

[89] "Towards A Theology of Religions: An Indian Christian Perspective," Statement of the Indian Theological Association, in *Religious Pluralism An Indian Christian Perspective*, edited by Kuncheria Pathil (Delhi: ISPCK, 1991), 336-337.

■■■

Towards Addressing COVID-19 Crisis: Re-Reading Cyprian's Responseto Suffering

Fr. Dr. Bijesh Philip

Introduction

Major gurus, philosophers, theologians, poets and other literary writers have tried to address the issue of suffering and to understand the meaning of life in the midst of human suffering. Even 'The Suffering Servant' raised a question at the peak of his suffering asking God the Father whether He had forsaken him. Some philosophers developed the 'Death of God' theory on witnessing the massive suffering and injustice in this world. Some others tried to help humans to avoid becoming victims of adverse situations by changing their thought responses to painful experiences. After the death of more than fifty lakh people in less than two years after being affected by COVID-19 and experiencing colossal planetary suffering, we who remain on this planet also naturally ask many questions about life and our world. Instead of just philosophizing or getting into a discussion on theodicy, the aim of this paper is to learn a few relevant insights from St. Cyprian of Carthage, a towering personality of the ancient Church, who witnessed massive sufferings due to the persecutions of Christians as well as the devastation caused by the plague.

Ordeal of COVID-19 - Some Facts

The novel corona virus or SARS-CoV-2 detected in China in 2019, which caused a respiratory illness known as COVID-19, spread rapidly across the globe. Most people did not have immunity against this new virus believed to have been transmitted from animals. The devastating effects of this highly contagious disease which affected all countries on this planet, continues to be unusual and horrifying. Globally, it led to a dramatic loss of human life, collapse of health systems, economic and social disruption and extreme poverty.

According to the WHO Dashboard, globally as of 11 November 2021, there have been 251,266,207 confirmed cases of COVID-19, including 5,070,244 deaths, reported to WHO. As of 10 November 2021, a total of 7,160,396,495 vaccine doses have been administered. Since all of us have experienced the pain of the demise of our beloved friends/ relatives, this is not just a piece of statistical information but an indication of a huge and unprecedented loss of life causing anguish to billions of people.

Across the globe, as part of safety measures, countries declared indefinite travel ban, sealing national and international borders, closure of educational institutions, worship places, entertainment centers, and commercial establishments including hotels and public transport. All countries imposed stipulations regarding the use of masks, physical and social distancing and frequent sanitizing. Avoidance of greeting by handshakes or affectionate hugs along with constant washing of hands have since become part of life. In addition to the grief over loss of life, the trauma caused by COVID-19 includes loss of community, missing worship services which sorely affected the elderly, loss of jobs and various financial problems, fear of getting sick and unprecedented physical distancing for long periods of time. The trauma of quarantine periods was also tremendous. Even after the development and use of vaccinations, many cases of people being affected, some even falling victim to death have been reported. Fear of mutations of the virus and the spread of delta variants is also rampant. One ray of happiness is that our previous envisioning of cyber churches is coming true in this situation. However, though virtual platforms and social media are used for pastoral care and worship, the faith of a few seems to be shattered. The most adversely affected people are the poor, the marginalized and the elderly. It is in this context, that the sufferings of Cyprian due to the plague and the persecutions in the Roman Empire and his response to them are being revisited for help and new insights to face the current crisis.

A Brief Sketch of the Life and Contributions of St. Cyprian

Cyprian of Carthage, a 3rd century saintly bishop, was a towering personality of church unity, discipline and mission. He was born and brought up in a family from another faith in the beginning of the third century. He used to serve as a teacher of rhetoric in Carthage, the most important ecclesiastical centre of the Roman province of North Africa. He embraced Christianity around 246 CE and within two years of his conversion he became a presbyter and the bishop of Carthage. He regarded Tertullian as 'the master' and read his writings daily. The scripture and the writings of Tertullian were the two major literary resources for him. As soon as he was appointed bishop, the Church had to face severe Decian persecution of 249-51. The Roman Emperor Decius planned to destroy the Church by liquidating first the leading bishops and then forcing all Christians to offer sacrifice to the Roman gods.

Bishop Cyprian had to address a huge controversy regarding the re-admission of the lapsed or the apostatized members of the Church. He gave exemplary and excellent leadership to the Church during this crisis.

He had great concern for the sick and suffering, especially the poor. A severe plague struck Carthage in the middle of the third century, and he rose to the occasion exhorting his people to alleviate the miseries of the sick and the dying. It was because of Cyprian's creative response to the plague which swept across the Roman Empire from CE 249 to 270, that it came to be known as the plague of Cyprian. Cyprian witnessed the devastating effects of this plague, at the peak of which the daily mortality was around five thousand. The specific purpose of his pastoral exhortation *On Mortality* which discusses the nature and the effects of this plague was in order to equip Christians to deal with the deadly endemic with hope and compassion. His treatises like *An Address to Demetrianus, Concerning the Works and Almsgiving* also bear witness to a creative response to this unexpected calamity.

This unique leadership came to an end when he was martyred on September 14, 258 during the Valerian persecution. Cyprian was the first African bishop to be a martyr.

Cyprian's creative responses to suffering

1. Accepting the reality of suffering

Pontius, the deacon of Cyprian, in his *Life and Passion of St. Cyprian* has mentioned a dreadful plague which invaded every house causing people to shudder and flee, discarding their dear ones infected by the disease.[1] Seeing this horrible picture, Cyprian compares the world to a collapsing house[2]and highlights the need of moving to a comfort zone viz.,the eternal abode.

Cyprian writes to the people of Thibaris concerning how to cope with the suffering that is a part of the Christian life: "But how grave is the case of a Christian man, if he, a servant, is unwilling to suffer, when his Master first suffered; ....If we suffer from the world's hatred, Christ first endured the world's hatred. If we suffer reproaches in this world, if exile, if tortures, the Maker and Lord of the world experienced harder things than these, and He also warns us, saying, "If the world hate you, remember that it hated me before you. ....If they have persecuted me, they will also persecute you."[3] The picture of Christ who went through sufferings and who is with those who suffer as highlighted by Cyprian is an enlightening thought to accept sufferings without frustration. He says that believers have the calling to follow the example of Christ here, before entering in to the glory of eternity.[4] As Lynchburg rightly observes "Cyprian tells of how Jesus Christ is one who is not only numbered with the prophets, but foretold by the prophets of His suffering and death."[5]

2. Inclusive nature without discrimination

Indiscriminate spread of the epidemic is highlighted in Cyprian's *on Mortality*. The epidemic was affecting all "without any discrimination in the human race, the just also are dying with the unjust."[6] He clearly says that as long as Christians are in the flesh they are bound to suffer like anybody else in this world.[7] Cyprian seems to correct a false notion that faith is a guarantee of protection from infection and mortality. He was fully convinced that plagues were inclusive without any special protection for Christians. Cyprian's deacon Pontius specially mentions that Cyprian was compassionate and concerned in word and deed about even the enemies and aliens during this crisis following the teachings of the Lord.[8]

3. Self-preservation and self-sacrifice

During the Decian persecution Cyprian withdrew to comparative safety. It was a quarantine or physical isolation from where he used to serve the Church. He might have thought that he could serve the Church better by departure than by death. His deacon Pontius thinks that it was providential to protect such a noble ecclesiastical leader so that the Church could be protected while going through a severe crisis. But when he was finally arrested and exiled during the Valerian persecution, he put aside all the suggestions made by his old eminent friends to withdraw from faith to save himself. Instead he willingly embraced martyrdom.[9]

4. Spiritual warfare and simple life

As taught by Cyprian, those who want to progress in spiritual life must make serious and continuous spiritual warfare against sinful passions and vices: "Our warfare is with avarice, with immodesty, with anger, with ambition; our diligent and toilsome wrestle with carnal vices, with enticements of the world."[10] There is also a battle with the sufferings and tribulations due to the onslaught of the plague. So Cyprian says "Let not these things be offences to you, but battles"[11] If the battle is won by being steadfast to faith, it will be crowned.[12]

Cyprian's treatise *The Dress of Virgins* written at the beginning of the epidemic, explains the need to lead a simple life by avoiding jewelry and cosmetics and all kinds of luxury. At the same time, he exhorts his flock to use wealth not for such vanities of the world but for good purposes like supporting the poor. For him Christian life is a lifelong struggle and progress through the narrow and difficult path as shown by the Lord: "By this pathway the martyrs progress, the virgins pass, the just of all kinds advance. Avoid the broad and roomy ways. There are deadly snares and death-bringing pleasures."[13]

5. Transcendence through faith and hope

Cyprian repeatedly teaches about the certainty of the joy of the ultimate hope as promised by Jesus Christ. Those who doubt Jesus and his words will be frustrated at the widespread high rate of mortality. Faith imparts the surety of the heavenly joy and Cyprian suggests that it is with this hope that the faithful have to face sufferings here. He reminds us to note how Jesus who was about to leave the world, strengthened the saddened disciples to rejoice because he would go to the heavenly Father. Based on this he argues that we should rejoice when our beloved ones depart this world.[14] He goes on to affirm Paul's words that,'death is gain because it liberates us from the suffering and enslaving passions in this world'. Faith and hope prepare the faithful to endure sufferings and struggle with patience like Job in the Old Testament and the Apostles and saints of all times.[15]

Cyprian's picturesque description of the ultimate heavenly joy based on Jesus' revelation and victory over mortality gives the inspiration to struggle onward in the present world. He portrays this ultimate vision as a calling to join in the eternal abode with the apostles, the martyrs, virgins and all those who were faithful to the Lord Jesus while they were in this world and had struggled hard facing many temptations and hardships. In the time of the epidemic he reminds the need of reflecting on the temporary nature of humans in this transient world because death "is not an ending, but a transit, and, this journey of time being traversed, a passage to eternity."[16]

In his letter *To the Martyrs and Confessors*, Cyprian encourages and lauds those who were confessing the name of Jesus Christ and enduring the suffering of torture and exile because of their Christian witness. In the same letter he says that their struggle in suffering is a proof of their faith in the Lord Jesus Christ who suffered and conquered the world and would stay with his followers in their battle of faith.[17]

6. Call for compassionate engagement

Cyprian thinks that disaster is a helpline to assess our humanity and a test to know who we are and whether we are sensitive to the suffering around us. In the context of the spread of the deadly plague, he thinks that pestilence and plague "call human race, to see whether they who are in health tend the sick; whether relations affectionately love their kindred; whether masters pity their languishing servants; whether physicians do not forsake the beseeching patients."[18]

Once Cyprian raised a large sum of money and sent it to the bishops of Numidia to ransom the captives under the Barbarian tribesmen who raided Numidia in CE 252. In his covering letter *To the Numidian Bishops*,Cyprian, quoting St. Paul, wrote, "If one member suffers, all the members suffer with it."[19] This vision of one family which prepares the ground for sharing resources for helping victims of poverty and injustice is seen in a deeper level in the writings of early Christian writers Basil the Great and John Chrysostom. For Cyprian, wealth or riches were not meant for selfish luxurious gratifications, but should be used in the light of the will of God. So he writes "Use them, certainly, but for the things of salvation; use them, but for good purposes; use them, but for those things which God has commanded, and which the Lord has set forth. Let the poor feel that you are wealthy; let the needy feel that you are rich. Lend your estate to God; give food to Christ."[20] Thus he exhorts the people to feed Christ by feeding the poor.

Scope of a creative response today in the light of Cyprian's teachings

Cyprian gave unique leadership to the Church during the time of sufferings caused by Roman persecutions and the deadly plague called Plague of Cyprian through his pastoral exhortations and life example. We have discussed a few significant insights available in his treatises which directly or indirectly deal with the sufferings and crisis situations which he and his community experienced in the middle of the third century CE in North Africa. Many of these still have the potential to help us face the Covid-19 pandemic which has enveloped our world around 1770 years after the outbreak of the plague discussed by Cyprian:

1. Intense and severe experiences of suffering shatter human over-confidence in the structures of our world which hitherto appeared to be solid foundations of life. The Roman Empire with its strong administration and powerful military had given security and peace (*Pax Romana*). With the unbridled spread of the epidemic, when people were confused, Cyprian was trying to draw the attention of the faithful to the unshakable and ultimate Transcendent foundation of life. Likewise, COVID-19 has shattered our absolute trust in the advances made in science, technology and economy. It must be noted that more deaths due to COVID-19, occurred in highly developed countries like USA in less than two years after its outbreak. It is also predicted that what the world experienced so far is a fore-runner of more severe, drug resistant new variants of the virus as well as that of future suffering due to technological crisis. Such situations demand an affirmation of steadfastness to faith as done by Cyprian to be successful in this battle of life.

2. Unimaginable suffering is an invitation to compassionate engagements with added vigor. Rather than a discussion on theodicy, one of Cyprian's priorities was to equip people to overcome the idolatry of self-preservation and to take care of the sick and the needy. Cyprian has even mentioned about the doctors who neglect the patients who approach them during the epidemic. Even when he draws attention to the joy of ultimate hope, he emphasizes the importance of taking care of the sick and the suffering, emulating the sacrificial love of Jesus and following his teachings. It was also a call to serve all without any discrimination. The current Covid situation also made many too self-centered and occupied with more Netflix and entertainments. True spirituality is a call for an effective balance between concern for one's own safety and compassionate concern for those who suffer around us and especially to be in solidarity with the poor in this crisis.

3. Each crisis gives a call for a thorough transformation. We have noted how Cyprian presents the plague as an invitation to give up hatred, greed, pride etc. and to overcome all kinds of enslaving enticements and luxury. His teaching to refrain from misusing wealth for luxurious gratifications but to use it for beneficial objectives like supporting the poor is the message for the plague of COVID-19 also. Corona virus has trained us to avoid unnecessary parties and to conduct marriages and other programmes in a simple way. When carbon emission was controlled by the restrictions regarding the use of vehicles and flights during the peak time of COVID-19, there was a rejuvenation of non-human creation. According to Cyprian, the reflection on the suffering and death associated with the deadly plague

raises a few enlightening questions for total transformation: "..whether the fierce suppress their violence; whether the rapacious can quench the ever insatiable ardour of their raging avarice even by the fear of death; whether the haughty bend their neck; whether the wicked soften their boldness; whether, when their dear ones perish, the rich, even then bestow anything, and give, when they are to die without heirs."[21] So, if dealt with properly, sufferings can liberate and transform.

4. Cyprian's unique initiative to guide the Church by being in self-isolation during the zenith of persecution, gives a guiding light to take innovative steps to nourish the Church during the time of unprecedented pandemic like COVID-19. Use of technology and virtual platforms for effective pastoral ministry especially during this crisis is extremely relevant. At the same time, it must be noted that later Cyprian bravely came forward to give in-person episcopal guidance and also to embrace martyrdom.

From a baseless blame game to a collaboration

An Address to Demetrianus written by Cyprian with an apologetic purpose helps us to see how Christians were blamed by the majority of other faiths for the wars, famine and pestilence they experienced. The accusation was that these sufferings came as a result of the failure of Christians to worship Roman gods. In his reply to Demetrianus, the Proconsul of Africa, Cyprian argues that actually the natural calamities and other sufferings occurred consequent to failure of the gentiles to worship the true God and because of their unjust persecution of innocent Christians. In his apologetic reply he goes to the extent of saying that the crises and sufferings were due to "the anger of an offended God."[22]Most of the time, these kind of attacks and counter attacks with a communal agenda develop when people suffer unexpected natural calamities. We witnessed how a particular minority community was targeted for the spread of this novel Corona Virus in India and how the Chinese were targeted in the West in the beginning. Science, as well as a healthier theology, are essential to address these kind of issues. Cyprian also blames old age and the decaying nature of creation for the outbreak of devastating calamities.[23]Like everybody else in his times, Cyprian was also unaware of the real causes that were behind the plague like unhealthy sanitary systems and bad hygiene. We need to count on the advanced science of our time as a divine instrument to analyze, understand and address the sufferings due to issues like COVID-19. What is essential today is a voluntary collaboration of the Church leaders with the civic authorities, scientists and medical experts for the greater good of the society, especially in times of crisis like COVID-19.

Wake up call for a brighter future

The devastating plague of Cyprian made him think aloud about the perishing nature of human life and the world, as well as about the obligation to serve the needy and the suffering. Likewise, the present crisis is also a wakeup call for seeing a 'new heaven and a new earth' in this world and the world to come which will empower us in our battles in adversity by being free from enslaving attachments. Faith is not rendered meaningless in the midst of the sufferings of the pandemic but is a powerful guide and protection to go through it successfully. Hope inaugurated by Christ who suffered in history, provides us with the power to transcend the present adverse situations also. But enlightened minds like St. Cyprian prevent us from confining his hope to self-preservation which seems to be the supreme priority of the secular world today.

{Fr. Dr. Bijesh Philip, an ordained priest of the Malankara Orthodox Syrian Church, serving as a professor in the department of Christian Theology at the Orthodox Theological Seminary and the Federated Faculty for Research in Religion and Culture, (FFRRC) Kottayam. His published works include 'Christian Faith and Global Peace' and 'St. Basil the Great and the Globalised India'}

Endnotes

[1] Pontius the Deacon, *Life and Passion of St. Cyprian* chapter 9 (https://www.newadvent.org/fathers/0505.htm Oct 11, 2021).

[2] Cyprian, Treatise VII, *On the Mortality* Chapter, 25 (https://ccel.org/ccel/cyprian/epistles/anf05. November 3, 2021).

[3] Cyprian, Epistles, 55.6.2-5.

[4] Cyprian, Epistle LXXX: To Sergius, Rogatianus, and the Other Confessors in Prison, 2.8. as quoted by Aaaron Glenn Kilbourn Lynchburg, in *JUSTIN MARTYR, IRENAEUS OF LYONS, AND CYPRIAN OF CARTHAGE ON SUFFERING: A COMPARATIVE AND CRITICAL STUDY OF THEIR WORKS THAT CONCERN THE APOLOGETIC USES OF SUFFERING IN EARLY CHRISTIANITY* (DOCTORAL DISSERTATION SUBMITTED TO THE FACULTY OF THE RAWLINGS SCHOOL OF DIVINITY, Virginia 2017) p.18.

[5] Ibid, p. 184.

[6] Cyprian *On the Mortality,* Ch. 15.

[7] Ibid, 8.

[8] Pontius the Deacon, *Life and Passion of St. Cyprian*, ch. 9 (https://www.newadvent.org/fathers/0505.htm Oct 11, 21).

[9] Ibid, Ch. 14.

[10] Cyprian *On the Mortality* , Chapter 4.

[11] Ibid, Ch. 12.

[12] Ibid, Ch. 13.

[13] Cyprian *On the Dress of Virgins*ch. 21.

[14] Cyprian *On the Mortality* Chapter 7.

[15] Ibid, Chapter 10, 11.

[16] Ibid, Chapter 22.

[17] Cyprian EPISTLE VIII.(6) *TO THE MARTYRS AND CONFESSORS* In the Epistles of Cyprian http://www.public-library.uk/ebooks/32/73.pdf P. 16.

[18] Cyprian *On the Mortality* Chapter 16.

[19] Cyprian, Epistle LIX.

[20] Cyprian, *On the Dress of Virgins,* chapter 11 (https://www.newadvent.org/fathers/050702.htm).

[21] Cyprian, *On the Mortality,* Ch. 16.

[22] Cyprian, *An Address to Demetrianus,* Chapter 5 (file:///D:/Cyprian%20An%20Address%20to%20Demtrianus%20Ad%20Demetrianum%20_%20EWTN.html as of November 15, 2021).

[23] Ibid, chapter 4.

■■■

Christian Witness and Pandemics - Shifts in Social Behaviour and Religious Culture

Rev. Dr. Joseph Daniel

"Is any sick among you? Let him call for the elders of the church; and let them pray over him, anointing him with oil in the name of the Lord: And the prayer of faith shall save the sick, and the Lord shall raise him up" (James 5:14-15)

Christian witness demands a participatory process: Christ's disciples, who make up the church, need to take part in the life journey of the community to cure the ills of the society in adverse situations. Adverse situations bring more challenges to the disciples to find more means and methods to serve the society. Pandemic crises in the world, the demand for the Church's social conscience and participation seems even more evident in the society. It urges the Church to take a participatory approach that goes beyond the ecclesial needs and focuses on people and purpose. It is in this context the pertinent question for the church today is how to show its ability to respond to unprecedented change in the society with both 'compassion to humanity' and purpose. When a pandemic or epidemic happens in the society, it demands social and behavioural changes in society. These changes in society create a problem of maladjustment within the society and when maladjustment occurs, the non-material culture including religion struggles to adapt to new material conditions. When the non-material culture struggles to adapt to new material conditions, the Church has a role to play in overcoming the struggle. It is important that the Church responds with compassion to the needs of society when a period of maladjustment occurs in the society.

In the light of this, what is attempted in this paper is a search to find answers to questions such as: How did the Church's witness during pandemics help to respond and adapt to the new material conditions? How did Church's witness during pandemics change the religious culture and social behaviour in society? The following analysis is an attempt to explore the ways in which the Church responded to world pandemics. It tries to formulate a viable witness model for emerging opportunities to bring about a positive change in the church and society in the period of the early Christian Church. It also addresses the additional accountability that the pandemic offers to Christian witness in the society.

Pandemics and Epidemics

There were more than thirty pandemics that affected the world badly in the past. Moreover, the epidemics also challenged the community living in those times. There is a distinction between pandemics and epidemics. A pandemic is a burst of global magnitude, and it happens when infection due to a bacterium or virus becomes capable of spreading widely and rapidly. It involves the spread of a new disease worldwide. However, an epidemic, though it has the potential to cause a worldwide spread, it remains limited to one city, region or a country.

The word pandemic comes from two Greek words – *pan* and *demos* – meaning 'all people'. Pandemic refers to a widespread epidemic of contagious disease throughout the whole of a country or one or more continents at the same time. [1] It is an epidemic happening globally, or over a very large area, crossing international boundaries and usually affecting a large number of people. The pandemics had led to unprecedented confusion throughout the world in all fields of life including religious life. Christians had to alter their worship patterns, day-to-day living and practices due to the widespread nature of the disease.[2]

Acts of the Apostles, Shepherd of Hermas, Justin Martyr's The First Apology, Letters of Dionysius of Corinth, St. Ephraim's writings and Cappadocian Fathers' writings give us glimpses of how far the early church fulfilled its mission in the care of the sick during the pandemic. It is also possible to learn about the changes brought about in the religious culture and social behavior in the society, through the incarnational model of mission during the first four centuries of Christian Era.

Church's witness of the care for the sick: A Catalyst to change the religious culture and social behavior

The early church considered pandemic situations as a viable atmosphere for the church to practise the virtues of generosity, openness and caring for the sick and the vulnerable in the society. Consequently, the Church attended to the needs of those who were quarantined, frightened and at risk in other ways with kindness and compassion. The following analysis will help us to find the evolution of a structured method of caring for the sick and a theology of healing in the early church.

From the writings of the Eusebius, it is evident that there was no organized system for the care for the pandemic affected sick people in the Greco- Roman World. Roman culture had not extended any kind of care to the infected people. The context of the ancient pandemic is self-explanatory in the writings of Thucydides (BCE 460-400) He Says:

> ...died like sheep. And this caused the heaviest mortality; for if, on the one hand, they were restrained by fear from visiting one another, the sick perished uncared for, so that many houses were left empty through lack of anyone to do the nursing; or if, on the other hand, they visited the sick, they perished . . . they perished in wild disorder. Bodies of dying men lay one upon another, and half-dead people rolled about in the streets and, in their longing for water, near all the fountains.[3]

This shows the sad plight of the pandemic affected community in the Roman Empire. The vulnerable predicament of the pandemic affected was beyond our comprehension as their dead bodies lay one upon another, and half-dead people rolled about in the streets and, in their longing for water, near all the fountains.The following statement of St Basil is self-explanatory of the condition of the pandemic that affected the Roman Empire.

> A great many found themselves trapped in utter destitution, without home or savings, without a family to support them, unable to find sufficient work to feed and support themselves. In rural districts a few might join the bands of robbers who preyed on travelers... It was a fate which awaited in particular the sick, the aged, the crippled, the blind, or otherwise disabled.[4]

Against this deplorable condition of total rejection of the pandemic affected, the early Christians introduced a counter-culture, which was radical and rooted in self-sacrificial love. This transformed the Roman culture and caused it to become a care giving community by introducing hospital care system in the Roman Empire.

Christian witness – An Incarnational Model

Any discussion about the Christian response to the pandemics rests on the Christian ministry as revealed in the life and mission of Jesus Christ. Ministry to the sick, the vulnerable and the marginalized has been central to the Christian ministry. "The Spirit of the Lord is upon me, because he has anointed me to proclaim goodness to the poor. He has sent me to proclaim liberty to the captives and new sight to the blind, liberty to those who are oppressed, to proclaim the year of the Lord's favour." [5]The Church considers the mission of Jesus Christ as a benchmark for the mission and ministry of the church. Consequently, the church sees it as her duty to affirm life and to equip her members to consider it their duty to risk their own lives for the sake of those suffering from sickness and marginalization. It was in this context the Church introduced an incarnational model of witness in the care for the pandemic affected in the society. The mission consequently appeared as a catalyst to change the religious culture and social behaviour in the society.

Since Jesus of Nazareth, healed the sick, the church endorsed the caring of the sick.[6]" Is any sick among you? Let him call for the elders of the church and let them pray over him, anointing him with oil in the name of the Lord: and the prayer of faith shall save the sick, and the Lord shall raise him up"[7]These instructions of St James were practised in the church in the case of the pandemic affected people. They introduced a culture of hospitality, generosity and sharing of resources. {The Church has been considering the mission of Jesus Christ as a benchmark for the mission and ministry of the church. Consequently the church has been seeing it as her duty to affirm life and to equip her members to see it as their duty to risk their own lives for the sake of those suffering from sickness and marginalization}repeated from the previous paragraph

It is reported that Roman Christians collected funds for the Corinthian church.[8] In the Acts of the Apostles it is recorded that the Antiochean Church collected money for Jerusalem Church. [9] Christians in Rome collected funds for the common good. [10] From the writings of Dionysius of Corinth and the writings of Justin

Martyr, it is evident that Christians had organized groups of local disciples to care for the pandemic affected sick. They organized and monitored the care of the sick and assisted in and funded burials, common meals, and other social services. Christians formed communities and helped manage risks. The new culture of the care for the sick had fuelled the emergence of a cultural and social change in the Roman Society.

Radical Christian vision of neighbourliness

A radical Christian culture of caring the pandemic affected in the Roman Empire seems to be an alternative Christian vision of neighbourliness that the Christians introduced. This is reflected in the words of Dionysius of Alexandria. He says;

> Most of our brother Christians showed unbounded love and loyalty, never sparing themselves and thinking only of one another. Heedless of danger, they took charge of the sick, attending to their every need and ministering to them in Christ . . . Many, in nursing and curing others, transferred their deaths to themselves and died in their stead.[11]

The aforementioned statement of Mar Dionysius reflects the nature of the ministry of the early Church to the sick. Bishops had given special instructions to the churches to care for the sick irrespective of their religious associations. For instance, Dionysius of Alexandria sent a letter to the church in Egypt extolling the worth of the Christians, of how Christians were compassionate to fellow Christians, even though they also became infected.[12]He taught the church that death caused by the caring of the sick was second only to martyrdom.[13]

It is reported in the writings of Eusebius of Caesarea about the attitude of the Christians to the people affected in an epidemic lasting from 312-313 CE le.

> For they alone in the midst of such ills showed their sympathy and humanity by their deeds. Every day some continued caring for and

> burying the dead, for there were multitudes who had no one to care for them; others collected in one place those who were afflicted by the famine, throughout the entire city, and gave bread to them all; so that the thing became reported abroad among all men, and they glorified the God of the Christians.[14]

This statement shows that the early Church had showed a counter cultural attitude to the pandemic affected people. Early Christians were successful in caring for those struck by an epidemic and their services were acknowledged by the public of the Roman empire as a counter cultural move from the Christians as there was no care giving system in the Roman empire and in other religious systems, which we have already dealt in this paper." In the classical world there was little recognition of social responsibilities on the part of the individual. Before the advent of Christianity, moreover, there was no concept of the responsibility of public officials in preventing disease or to treating those who suffered from it."[15] The most visible result of the Church's involvement in the care of the sick and the assertion of a new theology of healing had made Christianity a much more attractive belief system.[16]

> During these centuries the Christian faith . . . permeated all aspects of life in the West. The very conception of medicine, as well as its practice, was deeply touched by the doctrine and discipline of the Church. This theological and ecclesiastical influence manifestly shaped the ethics of medicine, but it even indirectly affected its science since, as its missionaries evangelized the peoples of Western and Northern Europe, the Church found itself in a constant battle against the use of magic and superstition in the work of healing. It championed rational medicine, along with prayer, to counter superstition.[17]

The alternate model of the care for the sick and the pandemic affected made Christianity a much more attractive belief system in the Roman Empire. The following actions of the Christian community had helped in expediting the process of social and behavioural change in the society. First, the early Christians had formed networks that provided hospitality, sharing of news, ideas, and texts and sharing of money. Second, Christian networks consider themselves as siblings.[18] Third, Christian disciples developed charity, an ethic of the care for the sick – A counter cultural move. Fourth, Christian disciples gave the hope that the disease is curable, Palliative care, provision for food and water could help recovery. Fifth, Bishops had given special instructions to the churches to care for the sick irrespective of their religious associations. Sixth, the Bishops taught the church that the death caused by the caring of the sick appears second to martyrdom, according to Eusebius,

> {Most of our brother Christians showed unbounded love and loyalty, never sparing themselves and thinking only of one another. Heedless of danger, they took charge of the sick, attending to their every need and ministering to them in Christ . . . Many, in nursing and curing others, transferred their deaths to themselves and died in their stead.}[19]This quotation is attributed to Dionysius of Alexandria in the Subsection which is entitled Radical ....

These words reflect that the early Christian witness was in line with the meaning of the word witness. The word 'Martyrs' translated as 'witness', belonged to a group of words: *Martyria*– act of witnessing; *martyron*–a testimony or a proof; and a *martyrein* – to witness.[20] Eusebius says:

> [For they alone in the midst of such ills showed their sympathy and humanity by their deeds. Every day some continued caring for and burying the dead, for there were multitudes who had no one to care for them; others collected in one place those who were afflicted by the famine, throughout the entire city, and gave bread to them all; so that the thing became reported abroad among all men, and they glorified the God of the Christians][21] This quotation is repeated verbatim from the previous page.

The aforementioned statements proves that the early Christians were successful in bringing a sense of neighbouriliness in society. Another instance was when an epidemic and famine broke out in Edessa, there was a hoarding of food supply in Eddessa. St. Ephrem organized a community to distribute food and care forthe sick, He also ministered to the victims of the plague and thus got infected with the plague resulting in his death in 373.[22]

Hospital Health Care System's Debt to Christian Witness

It was the Church which developed Christian communities to assist the sick and needy during the second century. Bishops, presbyters, deacons and deaconesses and the people of God continued their witness in the society by caring for the sick. Deacons and deaconesses focused on palliative care. Galen (131–201) a physician and his medical treatises formed the basis of western medicine for centuries. St. Basil of Caesarea founded the first hospital in 369 CE. This is the beginning of the modern hospital medical care system. In Constantinople, Alexandria, and throughout the Eastern empire, many hospitals were founded on the example of Basil's great "Basileum."Bishops in the eastern half of the Roman Empire begin to establish 'xenodocheia' as Christian welfare institutions for the sick and poor. Thus, the early Church introduced an alternate culture of inclusion and compassion for the sick in the Roman Empire. Moreover, the responsibility of the general public to care for the sick was a counter cultural move towards a radical Christian vision of neighbourliness.

Witnessing: A call to subvert conventional wisdom and culture.

Any discussion on Christian witness has its starting point in Jesus Christ, who was the epiphany of the Triune God. Jesus was the revelation of God, and God was in his very being. He was the image of God, the icon of God revealing and mediating the divine reality.[23] What he was like therefore discloses what God is like. Jesus is the model for Christian witness. To be a disciple of

Jesus means something more than being the student of a teacher. It is a call to follow Jesus Christ. For Paul, a disciple meant being an imitator of Christ. [24]To Bonhoeffer, "When Christ calls a man, he bids him, come and die."[25] His vision of life was moulded on the basis of shared culture, community spirit and the Holy Spirit. [26]Christian witnessing then can be understood as living intensely, living joyfully in celebration of life, because Christ came that we may have his life and have it abundantly.

Conclusion

In the light of this fact, let us look into the question of Christian witness in the context of the pandemic that seeks to define Christian witness in terms of changing values at the expense of communitarian values. Therefore, an insight into the basis of Christian witness and its life affirming culture of sharing would potentially be of considerable pedagogical and practical benefit for the church, as it would provide resources for the transformation of the society to affirm its responsibility to care the sick by their inclusion. Christian witness is rather a way of life, a way of living with Christ and working with him for transformation – both on the personal and corporate levels. Jesus' model provides a standard for Christian witness. It is a pilgrimage from Bethlehem to Golgotha and to the mount of resurrection. Fullness of life in Christ can be achieved by social transformation. The goal of witness is real transformation of the creation towards this fullness of life. By doing so, Christian discipleship, or witnessing through the church, can be a true leaven in a pandemic affected society to transform its culture from seclusion and isolation to a culture affirming the fullness of life. In short, the Church can serve as a catalyst to transform the socio-cultural and political systems through service to affirm life.

{Rev. Dr. Joseph Daniel is an ordained priest of the Mar Thoma Syrian Church, serving as a Professor and Research Guide in the department of History of Christianity at the Mar Thoma Theological Seminary and the Federated Faculty for Research in Religion and Culture, (FFRRC) Kottayam. He also pursues the post-doctoral Habilitation (Dr.Habil) research at the University of Bern, Switzerland.}

Endnote

[1] Mark Honigsbaum, *Living with ENZA: the forgotten story of Britain and the great Flu Pandemic of 1918* (London: Palgrave Macmillan, 2009) 1-11.

[2] Michael Flexseher, "How ancient Christians responded to Pandemics" in: *Oxford University Press's Bolg, May 2020, blog.oup.com/2020/05/how-ancient-christians-responded-to-pandemics/,*visited on February 9, 2021.

[3] Eusebius. Church history, book IX, In: Schaff P, Wace H, eds.,*Nicene and post-Nicene fathers, second series, vol. 1,* (Edinburgh: T and T Clark, 2009), 34-50.

[4] *St. Basil, Exegetical Homilies. Translated by Agnes C. Way, The Fathers of the Church, volume 46, (Washington, DC: The Catholic University of America, 1963), 83: Richard Finn, Almsgiving in the Later Roman Empire: Christian Promotion and Practice (Oxford: Oxford University Press, 2006), 20* -21.

[5] *Gospel of St. Luke 4:16-17*

[6] *Matt. 9; 10:8; 25: 34-26*

[7] *St. James 5: 14-15.*

[8] Dionysius of Alexandria was a Bishop of Rome from 28th December 248 until his death on 22nd March 264;*Letter of Dionysius of Corinth.*

[9] *Acts of the Apostles 11.*

[10] *Justin Martyr, Apology I.*

[11] Dionysius of Alexandria was a Bishop of Rome from 28th December 248 until his death on 22nd March 264.

[12] *http www.oxfordreferece .com.relay.rhodes.edu/view/10.1093/oi/authority,* Visited on February,9,2021.

[13] Michael Flexseher, "How ancient Christians responded to Pandemics" in: *Oxford University Press's Bolg, May 2020, blog.oup.com/2020/05/how-ancient-christians-responded-to-pandemics/,*visited on February 9,2021.

[14] Eusebius. Church history, book IX, In: Schaff P, Wace H, editors. *Nicene and post-Nicene fathers, second series, vol. 1*(Edinburgh: T and T Clark, 2009). 10-34.

[15] G BFerngren, *Medicine & health care in early Christianity* (Baltimore: Johns Hopkins University Press; 2009), 25.

[16] Rodney Stark, *Rise of Christianity, op.cit.,* 1-11.

[17] *Albert R Johnson, A Short History of Medical Ethics, (New York: Oxford University Press,2000), 1-13*

[18] *Letter of Dionysius of Corinth.*

[19] *Eusebius. Church history, book IX, In: Schaff P, Wace H, eds., Nicene and post-Nicene fathers, second series, vol. 1, (Edinburgh: T and T Clark, 2009), 34-50.*

[20] T W Manson, "Martyrs and Martyrdom", In: BJRL., 39 (1956-1957), 463.; *The New Testament Concept of Witness,* (New York: Cambridge University Press, 1977),7-8.

[21] *Eusebius. Church history, book IX, In: Schaff P, Wace H, editors. Nicene and post-Nicene fathers, second series, vol. 1 (Edinburgh: T and T Clark, 2009). 10.*

[22] *Kathleen E Mc Vey, "Ephrem the Syrian" in: Early Christian World, 1229; Philip Schaff and Henry Wace eds., Nicene and Post Nicene Fathers, 120-13; Doctor of the Church Eusebius. Church history, book IX, In: Schaff P, Wace H, editors. Nicene and post-Nicene fathers, second series, vol. 1 (Edinburgh: T and T Clark, 2009). 1.*

[23] Marcus Borg, *Jesus a new vision*, (London: SPCK, 1993), 1-5.

[24] *Letter of Paul to Ephesians 5: 1-18.*

[25] Dietrich Bonhoeffer, *The cost of discipleship*, (New York: Macmillian,1963),7.

[26] Marcus Borg, *Jesus a new vision, op.cit,* 1-10.

■■■

1

Globalisation of Media

Fr. Dr. John Thomas Karingattil

Globalisation is the most used lingo in contemporary political and academic debates. But it is a phenomenon as old as capitalism itself. The emergence of 'New Information Technology' facilitated the radical restructuring of capitalism, culture, media, and communication. This new transformation is an economic, political, technological and socio-cultural phenomenon. And its impacts are multi-dimensional. The existing global media system exhibits more economic, political and cultural imperialistic tendencies in content and style. This article deals with the question of globalisation and its linkage with media in the context of globalisation in a post-COVID era.

The term 'globalisation' was not coined until the second half of the twentieth century, but as a socio-economic process, it has a long tradition. The noun 'globe' in English is derived from the Latin globus and denotes a 'spherical representation of the earth.' The adjective 'global' began to designate 'worldwide' as well as 'spherical.' In the etymological analysis, globalisation refers to the globe. The verb 'globalise' appeared in the 1940s, together with the term 'globalism'. The word 'globalisation' first surfaced in the English language in 1959 and entered the dictionary two years later. Walters argues that in 1961 Webster became the first of major dictionaries to offer a definition of 'globalism' and 'globalisation'. Although the word 'global' is over 400 years old, usage of words such as 'globalisation', 'globalise' and 'globalising' did not begin until about 1960. The term globalisation was popularised only in the early 1990s (Robertson 1990; Giddens 1990). In the Oxford English Dictionary, the term appears only since 1992. According to the Oxford English Dictionary, the word "globalisation" was first employed in a publication entitled *Towards New Education* in 1930, to denote a holistic view of human experience in education.

The Human Development Report of the United Nations Development Programme (UNDP) argues that globalisation is not new. But the present structure of globalisation is totally different from its earlier versions. Since the 1990s, globalisation has become a major academic theme across disciplines, continents, theoretical approaches, and the political spectrum. The "Cold War Era" and the "Space Age" have been replaced with the "Era of Globalisation" in the age of "information revolution" and "computerisation". Different terms are used to denote globalisation. But each of these terms has different concepts and ideologies. From a media perspective, globalisation is the connectedness of production, communication and technologies across the world. Its operation mobilises through economic, political and cultural activities. Besides, it involves the diffusion of thoughts, practices and technologies. Thus, in the era of the global economy, global media enriches the spread of the ideology of globalisation. Though the term globalisation has an economic specificity, it has multiple dimensions. The economic globalisation can be measured in the four main flows such as goods or services, people or labour, capital, and technology. Anandam Kavoori argues that conceptual terms like modernism, postmodernism, capitalism, nationalism, postcolonialism, and terrorism are in some sense the logic of globalisation (2009: 6).

In this flow, media plays a vital and constitutive role in the social and cultural life of the people. In History of Globalisation in *Globalisation: Social Theory and Global Culture*, Robertson argues that the history of globalisation emerged before modernity and even before capitalism. He has mapped globalisation in five major phases such as the germinal phase (1400-1750), the incipient phase (1750-1825), the take-off phase (1825-1945), the struggle for hegemony (1945-1969) and the uncertainty phase (1969-1992) (Robertson1992: 58-60). The Industrial Revolution was a significant era in the history of globalisation which increased the quantity and quality of the products that led to higher exports, better trade and business relations. After World War II, the establishment of the United Nations was also a major step in globalisation. The promotion of free commerce and trade, abolition of various double taxes, tariffs and capital controls, reduction of transport cost and development of infrastructure, creation of global corporations, and the blend of culture and tradition across the countries created new conditions of globalisation. The actors of globalisation are the nation, state, individual, multinational enterprises, international organisations, and mass media sources. All these are influencing the process of globalisation in different ways. The driving force of globalisation is capitalism, industrialisation, and information and communication technology. According to Daniel Bell (1973), "today there is a transition from an economy of goods to the economy of information". The post-industrial society is based on an info-based society, where the production of information is the driving force. The end of the Cold War, the collapse of the Soviet Union, the transition from industrialism to post-industrialism, the global diffusion of democratic institutions and its interdependence have signalled the inauguration of a new world of the global community. The revolution of information technology has strengthened the ideology of enlightenment and modernity; it also resulted in the emergence of new forces of hegemony. In the globalisation process, the technological revolution has highly enhanced the global transformation in time and space. Thus, in globalisation, space is virtual, online, electronic, decentred, placeless and borderless. In the post-Covid era, cyberspace and virtual platforms are popular among common people and this cyber space is conquered by digital platforms, including Facebook, YouTube and Netflix, etc.

Definitions of Globalisation

There is no single agreed-upon definition of globalisation (Ferguson 2012: 17) and there is no consensus about the starting point of globalisation (Oommen 2006: 3). Academic debate provides huge bundles of definitions of globalisation. The following are some of the more frequently cited definitions of globalisation:

1. "It is the intensification of world-wide social relations, which link distant localities in such a way that local happenings are shaped by events occurring miles away and vice versa" (Giddens1990:64).
2. "Globalization refers to all those processes by which the peoples of the world are incorporated into a single world society, global society" (Albrow, 1990:45).
3. "Globalization as a concept refers both to the compression of the world and the intensification of consciousness of the world as a whole" (Robertson 1992:8).
4. "Globalization is a social process in which the constraints of geography on social and cultural arrangements recede and in which people become increasingly aware that they are receding" (Waters 1995:3)
5. "Globalization refers to the growing interconnectedness of different parts of the world, a process which gives rise

to complex forms of interaction and interdependence" (Thompson 1995:149)

All these five definitions are characterised by certain features of globalisation: intensification of global linkages; growing awareness of the global influences and increasing shrinkage of space and time. The first four definitions do not specifically mention the role of the media in the process of globalisation. Though Giddens provided the most neutral definition of globalisation, he does not mention the role of media and communication specifically in globalisation. But it reveals the worldwide social relations by mediation. Albrow says that people of the world are incorporated into a single world society. For Giddens, globalisation was an intensification of social relations; for Thompson it was interaction and dependency, but for Robertson it was the intensification of consciousness of the world. In this sense, Robertson takes a step further by referring to consciousness instead of social relations. Consciousness is already a more intensified experience of globalisation. The same view is shared by Waters. In fact, Thompson focuses more on the explicit role of media and communications. Many other definitions of globalisation are also debated in the academic sphere: Globalisation is the spread of "free-market capitalism (Friedman 1999:7-8). It is the "compression of the world and global interdependence" (Robertson 1992:8). Globalisation is a "social process" (Waters 1995) and a ""historical transformation" (Albrow 1996:88). Moreover, it is an "integration of market projects on a global scale" (McMichael 2000: xxxiii) and the expansion of market power as well as a domain of knowledge (Mittelman 2000). Thus, "globalisation is often seen as global westernization" (Sen 2009). According to David Held, globalisation is "the widening, deepening and speeding up of the worldwide interconnectedness in all aspects of contemporary social life, from the culture to the criminal, the financial to the spiritual." It consists of the multiplicity of linkages and interconnections that transcend the nation-state which makes up the modern world system (Ferguson 2012:17). In the globalisation debate acknowledged major changes in the 1970s (in finance, computing and economics), in the 1980s (the fall of organised communism and the end of the Cold War), and in the early twenty-first century (the terrorist attacks on the Twin Towers, the London underground and Mumbai) that intensified the process of globalisation (Beck 2000, Turner 2010: 9). Globalisation debate is varied in nature from decade to decade and discipline to discipline. It also varies from country to county and perspectives. But all the arguments have an interrelation with other concepts.

Globalisation has a strong connection with global media networks. Some of the dictionary definitions show the association of the phenomenon with media and communication. According to McMillian Dictionary "Globalisation is the idea that the world is developing a single economy and culture as a result of improved technology, communications and the influence of very large multinational corporations". Cambridge Dictionaries defines it as the increase of trade around the world, especially by large companies producing and trading goods in many different countries, and notes that the globalisation process is integrated with media and communication. The United Nations Educational, Scientific and Cultural Organisation's World Communication Report provides a powerful definition of globalisation as a "concept originating in Anglo-Saxon countries which refers to the increasing worldwide nature of industrial production and trade, caused by the rapid development of new information and communication technology, and the instant, planetary transmission of their content" (UNESCO 1997). Thus, globalisation is associated with de- territorialisation, social interconnectedness, and the speed or velocity of social activity. It is a long-term and multi-pronged process. Therefore, globalisation is a project and process of the global media networks and social media platforms.

Media and Globalisation

The early theories of globalisation are more sociological debates on economic, political, and cultural dimensions. But the latter part of academic debates argues that globalisation is predominantly the creation of transnational corporations and of the entire world as a 'global village' with a 'single market' for achieving maximum economic efficiency. The term, 'global village' describes how the globe has been contracted into a village by electronic technology and the instantaneous movement of information from every quarter to every point at the same time. It has later come to be identified with the internet and the World Wide Web. Thus, globalisation is viewed as 'global marketisation', competitive industry, and monopoly capitalism. The 'global marketisation' is based on the two pillars of 'privatisation' and 'liberalisation'. Ideologically, globalisation symbolises neo-liberalism supported by multilateral institutions. The linkage between globalisation and media has a lot to do with the transnational flow of communication through the press, radio, film, music, television, Internet, and other forms of social media. In this context, concepts like 'global village', 'global public sphere' and 'global civil society' emerged in global communication. The new information technology has conditioned media globalisation and laid the foundation for various aspects of globalisation. As noted earlier, Marshall McLuhan popularised the term "global village" in 1964 to describe the ability to connect and exchange ideas instantaneously in the age of the media. In *The Medium is the Message* he notes, "all new media are an extension of some human faculty" (McLuhan and Fiore 1967: 26). He refers to 'global village' as a global community existing with a level of connection associated with small rural settings. Hence, mass media and communication technologies are the primary instruments for cultural globalisation. Thus 'global village' means the world has been gradually coming under one umbrella and anything happening in any part of the world is making an impact on other parts. It has become a reality with the expansion of global capitalism and the market in the age of neo-colonialism and post-capitalism. McLuhan's idea of 'global village' clearly notes that the media has a major role to play in the process of globalisation. The link between globalisation and media has been indirectly acknowledged but studied by very few (Rantanen 2005:1). Rantanen says that in the academic debate on media globalisation, scholars have given only a little theoretical explanation for the interaction between globalisation and media (Rantanen 2005:17). This may have happened because most theorists of contemporary globalisation came from outside the field of media and communication studies. Besides, most media theorists have focused mainly on media economy, power relations, media impacts and inequality, etc. The primary vehicle of the phenomenon of globalisation is information and communication technologies. Globalisation and media are embedded in the process of transnationalisation of economics, politics, and culture. Moreover, Terhi Rantanen's study on media globalisation transcends the traditional media and globalisation theories. Terhi Rantanen rightly says that practically, there is no globalization without the media. Media globalization has aided in both the production and distribution of information which unifies widely different cultures and integrates them into one world. Thus, media globalisation is shaped by the connectivity of people, places, flows, and relationships. Marko Ampuja suggests that technological paradigm (media and communication technologies), the cultural paradigm (cultural imperialism), and the political economy paradigm (transformation of capitalism) are the major features of media theories on globalisation (Ampuja 2009:125). In fact, theories of globalisation enrich the analysis of transfer of technology, hegemony, and capitalism. Media, information, and capitalism have become the most dynamic features of the global market. Herman and Mc Chesney say that the globalisation of the market economy is not possible without global media and multinational media corporations, which act as the new missionaries of global capitalism (2000:59). They argue that satellite broadcasting and the World Wide Web have replaced colonial missionaries and settlers in promoting Western lifestyle and culture overseas. Today's globalisation era consists of variables like new markets, new tools, new actors, new rulers, and new ideology. All these variables operate through the media. New markets: foreign exchange and capital markets are connected globally and operating 24 hours a day; new tools are the internet-based social media networks; new actors are WTO, MNCs, IMF, etc.; new rulers are the multilateral agreements on trade, service, and intellectual property; new ideologies are based on neoliberal markets. Thus, from a media perspective globalisation process has a bright side as well as the dark side of market culture and fragmentation. The globalisation of media results in a higher percentage of media texts and content being reduced to the digital domain, and a new model of mass communication is unfolding. It is not one-to-many but rather, many-to-many. Users of Internet can post messages on websites; they can also create their own websites. These messages and sites can then be viewed by millions of internet users around the world. Therefore, media globalisation has aided both the production and distribution of information and entertainment.

Globalisation of Media

Media and globalisation are an integral field of communication that act as a single platform. They are interconnected and inseparable in both academic debates and public persuasion. Media globalisation is the phenomenon of expanding multinational corporate media investment, which own and operate a variety of mass media content and distribution technologies at a global level. The global media markets were established in the context of the neoliberal free market of the West in the late 1980s and 1990s. But its roots can be traced back decades. Since 2000, global media communication has shifted to digital transmission. Digital communication becomes the information superhighway open to all with the slogan of 'anything', 'anywhere' and 'anytime'. The internet revolution drastically transformed the media landscape to social media. The globalisation of media is embodied with the market and propaganda of products and ideology of the West. The twin hallmarks of neo-liberalisation and privatisation enriched the speedy spread of globalisation. The neo-liberal policies stimulated the commercial development of the global media. Herman and McChesney argue that the new information order of market freedom strengthened the global media system. The rise of electronic journalism and media literacy lead to a democratic revolution in society. In the previous periods, media content was written exclusively for a domestic audience. But the global news agencies were the "first significant form of global media" and its significant impact is felt on media globalisation. Now, the primary vehicle of the phenomenon of media globalisation is multinational corporations. It has aided in both the production and distribution of information and entertainment. Media Globalisation is also being driven by increasingly strong international market factors fuelled by organisations such as the World Trade Organisation (WTO), the International Monetary Fund (IMF), and the United Nations Educational, Scientific, and Cultural Organisation (UNESCO). Thus, media globalisation has been a natural extension of corporate expansion of WTO, IMF, and UNESCO. Therefore, globalisation is not necessarily a natural progression; rather it results from deliberate human choice by a powerful group of nations, transnational corporations (TNCs), and international organisations which have stakes in the process. The media and information technologies have provided methods for large corporations to maximise profits by entering foreign markets. The emergence of media globalisation is the result of the high speed in transportation, computerisation, media, and information technologies, which transform the spatial and temporal situations of human experience. Thomas L. Friedman has examined the impact of the "flattening" of the world and argues that globalised trade, outsourcing, supply-changing, and political forces have changed the world permanently, for both better and worse (2008: 49). In his book *The World is Flat* (2006) he describes how the world is becoming "flat" or globally interconnected, thereby allowing businesses all over the world to compete on a more equal playing field. Thus, globalisation is the process of increasing connectivity and interdependence of the global market and globalisation of media means that any person in any part of the earth can have access to the news through social media. The mass media or social media is generally considered as the major source of globalisation as a phenomenon and agencies of capitalism and cultural hegemony. Now globalisation is more intense, profound, and fast-moving. It is more dynamic than anything that has happened in a previous phase of human history. The emergence of 'media and information technology' facilitated the radical restructuring of capitalism with a 'single market'. The entire world is a 'global market' to achieve maximum economic efficiency. Media globalisation is a direct vehicle for the transformation of human lives and horizons. In the neo-colonial era, capitalism has metamorphosed into 'info-capitalism' or 'knowledge capitalism'. The center of gravity of new capitalism has shifted from 'production' to 'speculation' and the global economy has become a 'casino' with its inherent ethical deficits

(Kurian 2006: 223-235). Thus, the anti-globalisation movement, or counter-globalisation movement, is critical of the globalisation of corporate capitalism. The movement is also commonly referred to as the global justice movement. The alternative terminologies such as "globalisation with a human face" or "just globalisation" or "ethical globalisation" are anti-globalisation movements. The World Social Forum popularised the terms like "Asian globalisation" and "alter-globalisation". In fact, all these concepts are important for developing an inclusive and comprehensive intellectual framework of globalisation and media globalisation.

Conclusion

The basic character of globalisation is coercive and exploitative, and it is domination oriented. Globalisation is directed towards the concentration of power, information, wealth, and production and supply in the hands of a few rich countries and their TNCs. Though new communication technological advances are becoming more accessible to everyone, it has created an imbalance in the information flow. It unifies the patterns of communications around the world but the powerful business and political elites in each country are part of media interaction around the world. They construct news and views based on their political and market ideologies in cyberspace and technologies. In short, media and globalisation are interrelated and integrated into the lives of the people. The new information technologies facilitated the media to shape a 'global public sphere' and 'global market'. Social media provides a digital space where people across the world can communicate, regardless of time and distance. It also refers to the cross-cultural exchange of ideas and technology. Thus, media globalization is the worldwide integration of media and technology. It enhances the multiple flows of information and images between countries through global or digital media. Therefore, the new digital technology and media globalisation are some of the central driving forces of the church and society, besides global order, post-capitalism, and global market in the post-pandemic digital era.

{Fr. Dr. John Thomas Karingattil, an ordained priest of the Malankara Orthodox Syrian Church, serving as a Professor and Research Guide in the department of Christian Ministry and Communication at the Orthodox Theological Seminary and the Federated Faculty for Research in Religion and Culture, (FFRRC) Kottayam. He authored many books and articles.}

Endnotes

Albrow, M. (1990):Globalization, Knowledge and Society: Readings from International Society, London: Sage. Ampuja, Marco (2004) "Critical Media Research, Globalisation Theory and Commercialization", Javnost-The Public, Vol.11(3):59-76. Anthony, Giddens (2002): Runaway World: How Globalization is Reshaping Our Lives, London: Profile B Appadurai, A. (1996): Modernity at Large: Cultural Dimensions of Globalization, Minneapolis: University of Minnesota Press. Appadurai, Arjun (1990): "Disjuncture and Difference in the Global Cultural Economy" in Mike Featherstone, (ed), Global Culture: Nationalism, Globalization and Modernity, London: Sage Publications. Beck, Ulrich (2000): What is Globalisation?, Cambridge: Polity Press. Bell, Daniel (1973): The Coming of Post-Industrial Society, New York: Basic Books. Boyd-Barrett and TerhiRatanam (ed), (1998): The Globalisation of News, New Delhi: sage. Ferguson, Yale H. and Richard W. Mansbach(2012): Globalization: The Return of Borders to a Borderless World?, London : Routledge. Friedman, Thomas L. (2005): The World is Flat: A Brief History of the Twenty-First Century, New York: Farrar, Straus and Giroux Giddens, Antony (2002): Runaway World: How Globalisation is Reshaping Our Lives, London: profile. Held, David and Anthony McGrew, (ed) (2004): The Global Transformations Reader, An Introduction to the Globalisation Debate, (2nded), Cambridge: Polity

■■■

Pastoralia and Coping Skills in Long COVID Issues

Rev. Dr. L.V. Bipinlal

"World War III has begun. But for the first time, mankind is not at war with his fellow man. Countries are too busy battling an unseen enemy, a bug, a germ a virus known as COVID-19. How this war will end remains to be seen. How many lives will be lost, and when those who survive do so, how will the world prepare for the next pandemic? And rest assured, there will, beyond any doubt, be a next pandemic." (Thomas M. Malafarina)

Introduction

According to most of the world's leading transmittable disease experts, the Wuhan corona virus spreading from China is now likely to develop into a pandemic that circles the globe. Its prospect is overwhelming. Different variants of the virus create a lot of issues in human life. Coronavirus disease 2019 is not only the outbreak of a deadly disease but also affects the mental status of the population. People are confronted by fear, uncertainty, anxiety, unemployment, domestic violence and existential questions of faith. Nations across the world are taking drastic action against this deadly disease with strict lockdown measures, quarantines, school closures, travel bans, partial opening of the economy, sports season, gatherings and entertainment. Such a situation is unprecedented and has brought disruption of our normal life patterns and relationship. It has caused economic distress and even physical, psychological and spiritual problems. Post covid care especially the care of infected and affected people is a special area which needs more attention. Therefore, in this paper an attempt is made to understand the pastoralia (Pastoral response) towards long Covid or post Covid issues and coping skills.

COVID-19[1]

World health organization has given detailed information about the novel Corona Virus Disease (COVID-19). According to WHO it is an infectious disease caused by the SARS-CoV-2 virus. Most people infected with the virus will experience mild to moderate respiratory illness and recover without requiring special treatment. However, some will become seriously ill and require medical attention. Older people and those with underlying medical conditions like cardiovascular disease, diabetes, chronic respiratory disease or cancer are more likely to develop serious illness. Anyone can get sick with COVID-19 and become seriously ill or die at any age.

The best way to prevent and slow down transmission of the virus is to be well informed about the disease and the way the virus spreads. You need to protect yourself and others from infection by staying at least 1 metre apart from others, by wearing a properly fitted mask, and by frequently washing your hands with soap and water or by using an alcohol-based rub. Get vaccinated when it is your turn and follow local guidance.

The virus can spread from an infected person's mouth or nose in small liquid particles when he coughs, sneezes, speaks, sings or breathes. These particles range from larger respiratory droplets to smaller aerosols. It is important to practice respiratory etiquette, for example by coughing into a flexed elbow, and by staying home and self-isolate until you recover from feeling unwell.[2]

Long COVID (Post COVID-19)

If you have recovered from COVID-19 but are still experiencing some symptoms, you could have what is known as post-COVID condition. This is also referred to as "long COVID" sometimes.[3] Post COVID-19 condition, also known as "Long COVID," refers collectively to the constellation of long-term symptoms that some people experience after they have had COVID-19. People who experience post COVID-19 condition sometimes refer to themselves as "long-haulers."

While most people who develop COVID-19 fully recover, some people develop a variety of mid- and long-term effects like fatigue, breathlessness and cognitive dysfunction (for example, confusion, forgetfulness, or a lack of mental focus and clarity). Some people also experience psychological problems as part of post COVID-19 condition.

In the beginning Julio Torales., et al. published an article *The outbreak of COVID-19 corona virus and its impact on global mental health* in which they detail the published articles concerning mental health related to the COVID-19 outbreak and other previous global infections which have been considered and reviewed. In the last months, after the outbreak of a new coronavirus infection (COVID-19) on 31 December 2019 among humans in Wuhan (China), an increasing amount of information and concerns are impacting the global mental health. Global media, local and international health organizations (including World Health Organization), epidemiologists, virologists and opinion-makers put out information, recommendations and minute-by-minute updates on the spreading and lethality of COVID-19. Nevertheless, the burden of this infection on global mental health is currently neglected even if it may challenge patients, general population as well as the policy makers and health organizations and their teams.[4] But the situation has fully changed with studies showing that it affects not only physical health but also the areas of mental health.

Post COVID issues

These symptoms might persist from the initial illness or develop after recovery from the illness. They can come and go or even cause a relapse over time. Some of the post covid issues are given below:

a. Daily Activities: The outbreak of the pandemic brings about serious consequences. Apart from physical weakness, an emotional outbreak has to be contended with. This happens even to those persons who have not been affected by the illness. There is contentment that a crisis was avoided or prevented and at the same time fear that it might still occur. Both individuals and communities long to return to their habitual routines and totally banish the pandemic from their conscious thoughts. Post COVID-19 condition can affect a person's ability to perform daily activities such as work or the daily household chores. The main reason for this is the fear that has affected the people.

b. Fatigue : Fatigue means feeling overtired, with low energy and a strong desire to sleep that interferes with normal daily activities. It is not the same as simply feeling drowsy or sleepy. It is a situation in which one has no motivation or energy.[5] Fatigue is a frequent indication of many medical conditions that range from the mild to the serious.

c. Breathlessness : This is very common in people with a respiratory illness when afflicted with COVID. They get breathless both during the acute phase of illness and whilst recovering. Breathlessness can occur for lots of reasons, but it can often make people feel scared, anxious, even panic stricken which may limit their daily activities. Getting short of breath when walking up and down the stairs, finding it difficult to go for a walk, and often having to stop in order to 'catch' breath, feeling that breathing is really hard work causing the shoulders to heave as you breathe. One may find oneself getting tense and gripping things to help feel less breathless. One may also have the feeling of a tightness in the chest.

d. Cognitive dysfunction – Cognitive dysfunction refers to deficits in attention, verbal and nonverbal learning, short-term and working memory, visual and auditory processing, problem solving, processing speed and motor functioning.

e. Confusion: Webster's dictionary defines 'confusion,' as the failure to distinguish things. It is the state of being puzzled or unclear in one's mind about something.

f. Forgetfulness, or a lack of mental focus and clarity: For S.K. Mangal, forgetfulness is the loss, permanent or temporary, of the ability to recall or recognize something learned earlier. Forgetfulness is termed as the failure of an individual. [6]

g. Irritability: It is the quick excitability to annoyance or anger usually resulting from emotional tension, restlessness, physical indisposition, etc.

h. Reduced Consciousness: A lowered level of consciousness indicates a deficit in brain function. The level of consciousness can be lowered when the brain receives insufficient oxygen (as in hypoxia); insufficient blood (as in shock); or causes an alteration in the brain's chemistry. Decreased or impaired consciousness or alertness refers to decreased responsiveness to external stimuli. Severe impairment causes coma where the patient cannot be aroused. The eyes of a person in coma remain closed and do not open in response to any stimulation. When consciousness is decreased, the ability to remain awake, aware and oriented is impaired. Impaired consciousness can be a medical emergency.[7]

i. Anxiety: It is an abnormal state characterized by a feeling of being powerless and unable to cope with threatening events, typically imaginary. It is expressed by physical tension as shown by sweating, trembling.

j. Sleep disorder : **Sleep disorders** (or sleep-wake disorders) involve problems with the quality, timing, and amount of sleep, which result in daytime distress and impairment in functioning. Sleep-wake disorders often occur along with medical conditions or other mental health conditions, such as depression, anxiety or cognitive disorders. There are several different types of sleep-wake disorders, of which insomnia is the most common. Other sleep-wake disorders include obstructive sleep apnea, parasomnias, narcolepsy, and restless leg syndrome. Sleep difficulties are linked to both physical and emotional problems. Sleep problems can both contribute to or exacerbate mental health conditions and can be a symptom of other mental health conditions.

k. Neurological complications such as paralytic stroke, brain inflammation, delirium and nerve damage

l. Low mood: It is common to experience low mood after COVID. Feeling sad or empty for much of the time (one may feel worse first thing in the morning), becoming more tearful than usual, feeling irritable and intolerant towards others, losing interest in activities once enjoyed, finding it difficult to make decisions, paying less attention to appearance, having suicidal thoughts and death wishes.[8]

Coping Skills and post COVID issues

Coping skills are characteristic ways to deal with difficulties and influence how one tries to identify and solve problems. People who cope successfully not only know how to do things, but they also know how to approach situations for which they do not have readily available responses. As a consequence, they are less vulnerable. The coping skills that people have are related to their life experience like expectations, fear, skills, hope, etc., which influence the degree of stress they feel and how they cope with it. Experience and success are coping with similar situation with well-substantiated self-confidence. It is the ability to remain composed and "think on one's feet" instead of falling into pieces when faced with a problem.[9] All these contribute to the realistic appraisals of and response to situations.

Coping strategies act as actions to help people address stressful situations.[10] Coping strategies are classified as problem-focused or emotion-focused, and this classification is determined based on the behavioural and cognitive efforts used to address stressful encounters.[11]

Coping Process

Coping process or strategies are developed throughout the life of a person from childhood to old age through adulthood. Socialization and encountering various life situations help the individual in developing coping strategies. Attachment, developmental and coping experiences acquired throughout the lifespan are manifested in an individual's personality and in his ability to adjust his reactions in ways that reduce or enhance risk due to stress. If coping fails, it results in a variety of psychopathologies. The effectiveness of coping also depends upon social support. Psychopathologies may include the illnesses ranging from anxiety to more severe problems including neurotic and psychotic spectrum disorders.

Coping process or strategies are now recognized as distinct from defence mechanism.[12] Problem focused coping strategies are conceptualized as the strategies which include both cognitive and behavioural efforts to find the correct resolution for the problematic situation. Emotion focused coping include the strategic efforts oriented to make emotional responses or distressful reactions to the stresses of the outcomes of life situations.[13] Persons with problem focused coping use logical analysis and positive reappraisal at the cognitive level and seek guidance and support, and problem solving at the behavioural level. On the other side, persons with emotional focused coping use "cognitive avoidance and acceptance or resignation" at the cognitive level and "seeking alternative rewards and emotional discharge" at the behavioural level.[14]

People who generally cope successfully have a varied array of personal resources, which include the following abilities:

a. The ability to seek pertinent information

b. The ability to share concern and find consolation when needed

c. The ability to redefine a situation so as to make it more solvable

d. The ability to consider alternatives and examine consequences

e. The ability to use humor to defuse a situation.[15]

Pastoralia in Long COVID care

Pastoralia or pastoral works, in other words refer to the duties of a Christian minister. It refers to the pastoral care offered by a Christian minister. The usage of this word starts from the early 18th century. [16] The terms 'pastoral' and 'pastoral care' derive from the Latin word pastoralia, traditionally meaning to shepherd individuals who require caring acts that assist in their healing, sustaining, guiding, reconciling, and nurturing. It means empowering and liberating them in order to address issues and concerns arising in the context of their daily interactions. It refers to the pastor's concern for them in their search for the ultimate meanings of life.

Contemporary pastoral care has developed into a professional person centered holistic approach, recognizing pastoral/spiritual interventions such as assessments, support, counselling, guidance, education, and rituals to assist with the spiritual, religious, or existential needs of a service user.

The moral distress generated by COVID-19 is likely to be experienced by everyone, care providers and non-caregivers alike. Feelings such as guilt, failure and lack of worth at an existential level characterize moral distress. Attempts to help manage, work through, and let go of these feelings often fail because with moral distress, people are often unable to reclaim their own ego . They often feel unempowered and worthless. In such a state, what many people want, and need is someone to affirm their value. They seek someone whom they regard as more authoritative. Their positive transference often on such "authorities" cries out for validation and worth by simply taking on the role of forgiver.[17] Moral distress is an existential threat that, if not addressed, may challenge full recovery from trauma. The relationship between the mind and the body was highlighted in the interactions frequently strained and distressed in a time of pandemic.[18] Pastoral/spiritual care providers are often regarded in such roles, unconsciously exalted to the role of validator and forgiver. While other clinical providers help to confirm people's work and support their ego strength, they are not always regarded as validators of the essential selves of persons viz.,their souls. This reality often places spiritual care providers in a double role, wearing two hats. One hat is the trained and adept counsellor; the other is the transferred embodiment of one who has the power to remove guilt and affirm value.[19]

Pastoral Closeness in Physical Distancing

In many ways, COVID-19 has changed forever the way we interact as a society. Many national leaders have declared that

"We are asking people to come together as a nation by staying apart from each other." For the first time in living history, people were being asked to socially distance themselves for the protection of the other. This challenge for our society to adapt to a new way of living, working, and being was the backdrop for the more focused reality of healthcare settings where patients can no longer receive visitors, even if their condition was not COVID-19 related.[20]

For the Christian minister, models of pastoral ministry are of course drawn from the Gospel portrayal of the example of Jesus, who ministered to the most susceptible members of society, who went out to the fringes and who touched those who had leprosy, those who could not be touched. The question for the pastoral caregivers was how to integrate this model of pastoral ministry with the present day restrictions on our ability to "be with" the other?

I needed clothes and you clothed me, I was sick and you looked after me, I was in prison and you came to visit me. (Matthew 25:36)

COVID-19 could be described as the leprosy of modern days.[21] It has carried with it an air of stigma and fear. Those who have it are to be avoided, and interaction with people in general is to be very limited. This, of course, is necessary to prevent the spread of infection, but for the patient, it leaves them in a very isolated position at a time when they are at their most vulnerable. In the Garden of Gethsemane Jesus was alone pondering and worrying about what was to come. When patients are alone and isolated another level is added to their personal suffering. It is precisely at this moment that patients need others to "keep watch" and be with them in their moment of despair. One of the most pressing challenges for pastoral care is the puzzle of "how do we remain 'pastorally close while physically distant from patients with suspected or confirmed COVID-19'?"[22]

COVID-19 has posed immense challenges for society in general, and healthcare workers in particular. The impact and burden of the pandemic isolation on the emotional and physical welfare of patients and staff is well documented.

Coronavirus outbreak has challenged the whole world and the universal Church because it provides ample opportunity for mission work worldwide and to become the hands of Christ. The church needs to respond sensibly to the current situation and work, totally centered on the gospel. Everyone is talking about the corona virus, so why should the church remain silent and not offer solutions instead of bemoaning the current panic. The church is called to be the salt of the earth and the light of this world (Matthew 5:13–14).[23] Here are some practical things the church should do during this time of worldwide panic.

a. Strengthening mental and spiritual health, well-being and resilience, through individual contact (while observing appropriate physical distancing) and through social and other media of communications.

b. Diligently address/educate the congregation on the issue of stigma, violence, and the incitement of hate because of COVID-19.

c. Spread awareness about sharing accurate information with communities and counter misinformation.

d. Provide help to those who need assistance (physical, financial, medical and spiritual). Faith communities can identify ways that their members can help others (checking on the elderly, people with disabilities, and vulnerable neighbors by phone and offering to deliver groceries, etc.).The church can promote the sharing of resources to provide for those whose livelihoods are disrupted and who cannot provide for themselves and their families.[24]

The severity of the disease caused by the Corona Virus is unnerving and cause a rise in anxiety verging on panic. Alongside the government appointed agencies, ministers, chaplains, counsellors and educators can accompany people passing through this valley of anxiety, fear, and death. Caregivers belonging to these categories become more important and crucial in the fight to overcome this pandemic and long covid.

Religious leaders and faith communities play a unique role in creating relationships and connections between people across age groups, professions and neighborhoods. In such a distressing time as this, pastoral care and counselling become more important and vital than at any other time. Pastors are called to maintain and strengthen relationships at this time even more than at other times as it can fortify the mental and spiritual health of their members and followers and contribute to the resilience of the larger community. Practices such as prayer, inspirational reading, and safe community service can build confidence and create a sense of calm.[25]

Listen in love. No matter what turn a crisis takes, one of the most enduring and powerful gifts we can offer is to listen. By listening we embody the love of the sacred, the love of a wider community, the love of life itself. Compassionate listening is exactly what people need when they are faced with the overwhelming, uncontrollable circumstances of a crisis. Pastors must not think only of their members but must be willing to listen to all needy people irrespective of race, religion, creed and gender.[26]

Provide comfort and hope to the afflicted and suffering: Offering special prayers for the sick along with messages of hope and comfort is obligatory for every pastoral care-giver. However, with uncertainties looming over the availability of vaccines, the afflicted are becoming hopeless and anxious with each passing day. Pastors can provide such people and their faith communities with appropriate prayers, theological and scriptural reflections and messages of hope. Highlighting the opportunities presented for reflection, prayer, and time with family members and others can also prove helpful.

Essential elements of *Pastoralia*

In *pastoralia* these are five essential elements which are very important for the optimal physical and mental wellbeing required for COVID and long covid patients. In their nature and scope they are apt in pastoral care towards long COVID.

***i. Pastoralia is a face of human concern through activities*:** It is the declaration of the nature of activity. Various helping activities such as counseling may offer such an expression but so are celebrating, commemorating, rejoicing and reflecting, as well as mourning or being present with people at different stages of life. [27]

ii. Pastoralia recognize transcendence: People who participate in pastoral care recognize a transcendent dimension to life. They realize that there is more to life than often meets the eye. They have awareness that power, grace and goodness are often not found in the obvious places. They recognize that there is a mystery, a mysticism about life, which is not reducible to sociological, psychological or physiological analyses and explanations. This transcendence is real, although we have no objective and external means of gaining access to it and of verifying whether we are right or not.[28]Psychologist Linda Myers,[29] describes this conceptual system as 'optimal psychology' according to which 'self knowledge is the source and basis of all knowledge'.[30] Recognize transcendence and be prepared to examine the implications of transcendence for the particularities of daily human living.

***iii. Pastoralia entails multivariate forms of communication*:** Oral communication is very important by which information is expressed and established. On the other hand, the non-verbal communication is more and more accepted as a powerful mode of communication, conceivably even of superior significance than the oral. In many cultures, indirect forms of conversing are very highly valued. In intercultural pastoral care, the forms of communication present in any given society are explored to ascertain their value within the society for caring interaction. Reading in between the lines is the main focus.

***iv. The motive is love*:** At the heart of the 'hiddenness' of (Pastoralia) pastoral care is love. In Christian terms, 'we love because God first loved us' (1John4:19). Love is a thoroughly social phenomenon. Not only does it impel us into relationship with others, but it also enables us to recognize injustice and to desire to do something about it. Christianity points to agape, referring to the unconditional self-giving love of God, as the source and sustainer of the universe. In intercultural pastoral care, love is both the motivation and the motive force.[31]

***v. Pastoralia aims at prevention and fostering*:** Pastoral care also aims at preventing distress where possible, by creative anticipation and sensitive, non-intrusive awareness-building. This is an educative exercise of pastoral care which enables people imaginatively to explore and examine situations before they occur in order to be prepared if they were to happen. Pastoral caregivers, in this view, are also deeply involved in fostering or enabling human growth and the fulfillment of the potential of individuals as well as communities.[32] Application of these elements helps the long covid person to face the challenges and to overcome the situation.

Conclusion

Pastoralia (Pastoral care) for Long COVID or post COVID issues is the pressing need of the society at large. Coping skills are essential to face the challenges. The role of faith community in the midst of this situation is remarkable. The healing of a COVID patent is incomplete, even though he is diagnosed as negative, because it affects not only the physical realm but also the psyche and soul. Through these mediums one can strengthen mental and spiritual health, well-being and resilience, by contacting COVID patients individually using social and other media of communications. *Pastoralia* aims to accomplish the health and wholeness of the world in its fullness.

{Rev. Dr. L. V. Bipinlal, an ordained priest of the Church of South India, is the Treasurer of FFRRC. He is specialised in the branch of Pastoral Care and Counselling and authored many books and articles. Currently he serves as the Professor in the department of Christian Ministry at Kerala United Theological Seminary, Thiruvananthapuram and FFRRC, Kottayam}.

Endnotes

[1] Coronavirus disease (COVID-19), https://www.who.int/health-topics/coronavirus#tab=tab_1, 24/2.2022, 10.05 pm.

[2] Coronavirus disease (COVID-19), https://www.who.int/health-topics/coronavirus#tab=tab_1, 24/2.2022, 10.05 pm.

[3] Vismita Gupta-Smith, *Post COVID-19 condition https://www.who.int/emergencies/diseases/novel-coronavirus-2019/media-resources/science-in-5/episode-47—post-covid-19-condition?gclid=Cj0KCQiA3-yQBhD3ARIsAHuHT66J3UtKgjpdok_B1LhS8Zsk0NnYTzm3LNbRD_Qgy-8EtwEvvPYfDxsaAiBaEALw_wcB 27/2/22 11.28pm.*

[4] Julio Torales. "The outbreak of COVID-19 corona virus and its impact on global mental health" International journal of social psychiatry (1-4) (2020), 1.

[5] Krista O'Connell *Causes of fatigue and How to manage it* https://www.healthline.com/health/fatigue uploaded on March 29, 2020 and accessed on 6/3/2022 5.17pm

[6] S.K. Mangal, *An introduction to psychology* (New Delhi: Sterling Publishers, 2012), 151.

[7] Verneda Lights, https://www.healthline.com/health/consciousness-decreased Updated on September 18, 2019, accessed 7/3/22

[8] Managing your mood and coping with frustration, https://www.yourcovidrecovery.nhs.uk/managing-the-effects/effects-on-your-mind/managing-your-mood-and-coping-with-frustration 7/3/2022

[9] Irwin G. Sarason, Barbar R. Sarason. *Abnormal Psychology – the problem of maladaptive behavior eleventh edition* (New Delhi: PHI Learning Private Liomited, 2010), 159.

[10] Zamira Hyseni Duraku and Linda Hoxha. "Self-esteem, study skills, self-concept, social support, psychological distress, and coping mechanism effects on test anxiety and academic performance," *Health Psychology Open (*July-December 2018): 1. (1 –9)

[11] Zamira Hyseni Duraku and Linda Hoxha. "Self-esteem, study skills, self-concept, social support, psychological distress, and coping mechanism effects on test anxiety and academic performance,".....

[12] Daniel Burnabas *Distant Half Distress Heart Stress of wife in relation to prolonged Absence of Husband* (Delhi: SATHRI/ISPCK, 2008), 36.

[13] Suzette Boon, Kathy Steele and Onno Van Der Hart *Coping With Trauma-Related Dissociation Skills Training for Patients and Their Therapists* (Now York : W.W. NORTON & COMPANY, 2011), 253.

[14] R. H. Moos *Coping Responses Inventory: CRI from Adults. Professional Manual,* (Odessa: Psychological Assessment Resources, 1993), 45.

[15] Irwin G. Sarason, Barbar R. Sarason. *Abnormal Psychology – the problem of maladaptive behavior eleventh edition..., 159-160.*

[16] L.V. Bipinlal, *StressTolerance, Co-Dependency, Self-esteem Pastoralia Revisited* (ISPCK and Kerala United Theological Seminary, 2022), xv.

[17] Terry R. Bard, "COVID-19 and a New Normal?" *Journal of Pastoral Care & Counseling* 74/2 (June, 2020), 81.

[18] Drummond, D. A., & Carey, L. B. "Chaplaincy and Spiritual Care Response to COVID-19: An Australian Case Study – The McKellar Centre." *Health and Social Care Chaplaincy,* 8/2, (2020) 169. (165–179)

[19] Terry R. Bard, "COVID-19 and a New Normal?"..., 81.

[20] Byrne, M. J., & Nuzum, D. R.. Pastoral Closeness in Physical Distancing: The Use of Technology in Pastoral Ministry during COVID-19. *Health and Social Care Chaplaincy,* 8/2,(2020), 206–217.

[21] M. J., & Nuzum, D. R.. Pastoral Closeness in Physical Distancing: The Use of Technology in Pastoral Ministry during COVID-19..., 211.

[22] D. Nuzum. "The COVID-19 dilemma: How to maintain physical distance without sacrificing pastoral closeness," *SEARCH*, 43/2, (2020), 105. (104-107).

[23] Ken Ham, "Coronavirus: Opportunity for the Church to Be the Hands of Christ," *Answers in Genesis*, https://answersingenesis.org/coronavirus/coronavirus/ (2 Oct 2020).

[24] Practical considerations and recommendations for religious leaders and faith-based communities in the context of COVID-19: Interim Guidance (7 April 2020), *World Health Organization*, 1-4. https://www.who.int/publications/i/item/practical-considerations-and-recommendations-for-religious-leaders-and-faith-based-communities-in-the-context-of-covid-19 (3 Oct 2020).

[25] Practical considerations and recommendations for religious leaders and faith-based communities in the context of COVID-19: Interim Guidance (7 April 2020)…, 4.

[26]Eileen R. Campbell-Reed, 10 guidelines for pastoral care during the coronavirus outbreak (10 March 2020), *The Christian Century,* 2, https://www.christiancentury.org/blog-post/guest-post/10-guidelines-pastoral-care-during-coronavirus-outbreak (3 Oct 2020).

[27] Emmanuel Y. Lartey, *In Living Color An Intercultural Approach to Pastoral Care and Counseling Second Edition* (London: Jessica Kingsley Publishers, 2003), 27-28.

[28] Emmanuel Y. Lartey, *In Living Color An Intercultural Approach to Pastoral Care and Counseling Second Edition...*

[29]Linda James Myers. Understanding an Afrocentric World View: Introduction to an Optimal Psychology. Dubuque: Kendall/Hunt Pub.co, 1993), 10.

[30] Emmanuel Y. Lartey, *In Living Color An Intercultural Approach to Pastoral Care and Counseling Second Edition...,*

[31] Emmanuel Y. Lartey, *In Living Color An Intercultural Approach to Pastoral Care and Counseling Second Edition...,30.*

[32] Emmanuel Y. Lartey, *In Living Color An Intercultural Approach to Pastoral Care and Counseling Second Edition...,* 31.

■■■

Reminiscences of the Federated Faculty for Research in Religion and Culture

Rev. Dr. M.J. Joseph

"Think globally and act locally"

I congratulate the FFRRC administration in its attempt to bring out a volume with the title "Towards a Relevant Ministry in the Post-Pandemic Period: Biblical, Theological, Historical, Missional, Ministerial Perspectives" to commemorate the Ruby Year of FFRRC's role in theological education under the Senate of Serampore University. I am indeed grateful to the Registrar, Rev. Dr. Koshy P.Varughese, for requesting me to contribute an article regarding the genesis of FFRRC in my capacity as the first Registrar of the FFRRC. The FFRRC was indeed a new experiment in Ecumenism and it was inaugurated on July 3, 1980 at Kottayam in the presence of an august assembly.

I am reminded of the Chinese proverb which says that a journey of a thousand miles begins with the first step. Yes, the formation of FFRRC was indeed a local initiative in ecumenism under the stewardship of three theological colleges of Kerala- the Orthodox Theological Seminary, Kottayam, the Mar Thoma Theological Seminary, Kottayam and the Kerala United Theological Seminary, Trivandrum.

As excellence in theological education is not negotiable, it was imperative for the theological colleges in India to explore new avenues in theological education with contextual relevance. The search for vision and focus on theological education was indeed an ongoing discussion during the last several decades under the Serampore system. In the well -known Ranson Report of 1945, it was affirmed that the cultural context, natural gifts, talents and capacities of the candidates for the ministry must be fully recognized in the process of theological education. The Harrison Report in turn gave priority to the forms and the tasks of the Christian ministry in each cultural context. The formation of FFRRC is the realization of theological education in the pluralistic context of the country with local relevance.

A page from history

The possibility of setting up a post graduate theological Faculty in Kerala was raised by the then Director of the Senate Prof. Dr. T.V.Philip in a meeting of Young Theologians' Conference under the Research Department of the Senate at Kottayam in July 1977. In response to his appeal, an exploratory committee was formed with Rev.Dr.M.J.Joseph as its Convener. The first meeting of the exploratory committee consisted of delegates from St. Thomas Apostolic Seminary, Vadavathoor, Orthodox Theological Seminary, Kottayam, Mar Thoma Theological Seminary, Kottayam and Kerala United Theological Seminary, Trivandrum. The main objective of the meeting was to explore the possibilities of the pooling of all the theological resources in Kerala for a post graduate programme and research. All the delegates actively participated in the discussions regarding the realisation of the above objective. Since then, the exploratory committee met several times and formulated rules and regulations for the Federated Faculty.

The purpose of the Federated Faculty as stated in the original application to the Senate is given below:

1. To promote research in disciplines connected with religion and culture leading to the master's and doctor's degree of the Senate.

2. To promote facilities for advanced research, not necessarily leading to a degree.

3. To promote the study of Church traditions in depth considering the secular, religious and ecumenical contexts in India.

4. To promote a forum for creative dialogue between religious and secular thinkers.

5. To provide facilities for the teaching of classical languages like Hebrew, Greek, Sanskrit, Latin and Syriac as well as modern languages like German and French.

Besides the above, the following objectives were included at a later stage.

(a) To provide scope for the training of resource persons for the mission of the Church and to strengthen the life of the Church and congregations through a deeper understanding of their mission and life.

(b) To provide for greater interaction among the Churches and a greater involvement in their theological thinking.

(c) To provide scope for greater co-operation among the sister seminaries particularly in the matter of research and study at regional levels.

(e) To ensure greater co-operation at the post-graduate level of studies without a "centralized structure".

From the above objectives, it is obvious that the FFRRC does not envisage the setting up of a Study Centre at a new place. The co-operation is extended in the area of sharing the faculty and library resources of the Federated Colleges for study and research. This perspective of the FFRRC was warmly received in the ecumenical circles. The formation of the FFRRC created ripples all over India and in the meeting of the Congress of Asian Theologians (CATS). This pattern has been followed in other regions too. In my article on SATHRI when it celebrated its Silver Jubilee, I had made mention of the importance of FFRRC as "a great ecumenical milestone."(Silver Jubilee Special edited by Dr.P.G.George-Sept.2014, p.104). I have had several occasions to make mention of the ecumenical legacy of FFRRC to several of the SATHRI candidates while I was serving the SATHRI (**South Asia Theological Research Institute**) as its chairman for a term.

FFRRC taking off

On May 14, 1979, the exploratory committee under the chairmanship of Dr. Paulose Mar Gregorios, Principal, Orthodox Theological Seminary and the concurrence of the other two Principals, resolved to request the Senate to grant affiliation for M.Th. courses in Old Testament, New Testament and Christian Theology. All the required details along with the application signed by Dr. Paulose Mar Gregorios, Rev.Dr.V.P.Thomas, Principal, Mar Thoma Theological Seminary and Rev.Dr.Jacob Verghis, Principal, Kerala United Theological Seminary, Trivandrum, were submitted to the Registrar of the Senate on May 17,1979.Rev.Dr.M.J.Joseph, the Convener of the Committee, had the difficult task to get the procedural niceties cleared for the approval of the Mar Thoma Church through its Sabha Council and later at the level of the *Prathinidi Mandalam.* The Committee formulated the rules and regulations for the functioning of the FRRRC. It was decided to locate the office of the Registrar's office at the Mar Thoma Theological Seminary, Kottayam and Rev. Dr. M.J. Joseph, the Convener of the Committee, was requested to serve as its Registrar and the three Principals of the Federated Colleges were asked to continue as the co- chairpersons of the FFRRC for a term of three years. Later the Committee on Academic Administration of the Senate sent Dr.P.V. Premsagar (President of the Senate),Dr. K. James Carl, Dr.C. Duraisingh and Rev.D.S. Sathyaranjan (Registrar) to visit the Federated College for further evaluation. In its meeting of the Senate of Serampore College held on Feb.1, 1980, at the Tamil Nadu Theological Seminary, the FFRRC was recognized and affiliation at the M.Th. level was granted.

The official inauguration of the FFRRC was held on July 3, 1980 at the M.T.Seminary High School auditorium. Prof. Sukumar Azhikode was the main speaker. A Souvenir edited by Fr.Dr.K.M.George, a faculty member of the FFRRC, was published on the occasion. The messages received from H.H.Baselius Mar Thoma Mathews I, Catholicose of the East, Dr. Alexander Mar Thoma Metropolitan, Rt.Rev .I.Jesudason, C.S.I and Prof. Dr. M.V.Pylee, Vice-Chancellor, University of Cochin were indeed valuable. The presence of the heads of the churches, the Principals of the Federated Colleges, faculty members, students and a good audience from different churches made the occasion memorable. The newly elected Principal of the Mar Thoma Theological Seminary, Rev. Dr.K.C.Mathew was also present.

A leap into the unknown

Doing Asian Theologies in the context of God 'oikos' is being realized with the launching of the FFRRC. The initiative of the seminaries was welcomed by the members of the respective churches of federated colleges .The first batch of students (as per the Souvenir1980-'81 were Mr. Daniel George (NT), Mr. Moses

Luke, Rev. Fr. K.I. Mathew Vaidyan and Rev. R.C. Thomas (ChristianTheology), Rev. C. Russeliah, Rev. A. Ganadason and Fr. T.P. Mathew (For their qualifying examinations). The faculty members in the early period included Dr. K.V. Mathew, Dr. K.A. George and Fr. K.M. Alexander(OT); Dr. Jacob Verghis, Dr. M.J. Joseph Fr. George Kaniarakath and Fr Dr. Mathew Vellanickal (NT) Dr. Paulose MarGregorios, Dr. V.P. Thomas, Dr. K.M. George, Dr. K.C. Mathew, Dr. P.G. Kuruvilla, Dr. V.C. Samuel(Christian Theology). Later, other areas of study at the M.Th. level were added according to the availability of the teaching staff in the federated colleges. The candidates had the privilege of making use of the library facilities of the Federated Colleges and of the St. Thomas Apostolic Seminary, Vadavathoor.

Rev. Dr. M.J.Joseph served as the Registrar of the FFRRC from 1980-1986 and later as one of the Chairpersons from 1989-1991. He was also one of the speakers at the Silver Jubilee Celebrations of the FFRRC with Dr. P.L.John Panicker as its Registrar. His Lordship the Late Bishop Geevarughse Mar Athanasius was the main speaker on that occasion.

The students for the M.Th. and D.Th. programmes under FFRRC were given the option to stay in any of the Federated colleges during the period of their study. It was indeed remarkable that Rev.R.C.Thomas of the Mar Thoma Church stayed at the Orthodox Theological Seminary for two years and participated in the life of the Seminary . The FFFRRC is indeed proud of Rev. Dr..R.C.Thomas (Mar Thoma) and Fr.Dr.Regi Mathew (Orthodox) who later pursued their doctoral studies in Germany. Dr.R.C.Thomas had the privilege to do his ***doctor arbeit*** under the supervision of Dr.Konrad Raiser who later became the General Secretary of the WCC.

The federated colleges provided single accommodation for the students. Several of the candidates who had completed their M.Th. under the FFRRC did their doctoral programme either in India or abroad. A few of them joined the faculty of their own theological colleges. The candidates were given the option of finding their own accommodation in any of the seminaries or elsewhere. Within a few years quite a number of students from all over India across denominational barriers particularly from the Northeast India joined the FFRRC for the M.Th. and D.Th. programmes of the Senate. A few women candidates also joined the FFRRC for their post- graduate and doctoral level research programmes.

Concluding Remarks

It is indeed an honour that the Registrar of the FFRRC is invited to attend the annual meetings of the Board and the Convocation meeting of the Senate of Serampore College. As a sign of FFRRC's ecumenical commitment the faculty and the students spend two or three days every year for an in-depth theological discussion on a relevant topic at the Ecumenical Christian Center, Bangalore. It was first organized while I was the Director of the Ecumenical Christian Centre. In its early period, the Registrar of the FFRRC had an office at C.V.John Memorial Administrative Block at the MTT Seminary. After a few years of its presence at the OTS, the office is now re-located at the new office block of the Mar Thoma Theolgical Seminary and functioning with the FFRRC office staff. There was an attempt to build a small library in the FFFRRC office on subjects dealing with the history and culture of Kerala during my tenure as its Registrar. But the initiative did not take off. The FFRRC used to conduct an essay competition for a few years as a mark of its involvement in the cultural context of India. An endowment was set up to award prizes to the winner. That effort too did not flourish in later years.

As we reflect on the relevance of ministry in the post--pandemic period during the Ruby year of the FFRRC, we should remember that the challenge of the 'New Normal' is to be pursued by the Federated Colleges in its academic programmes.

{Rev. Dr. M.J. Joseph, the First Registrar of the FFRR , was formerly the professor of NT and Principal of the Mar Thoma Theological Seminary, Kottayam and the Director of the Ecumenical Christian Center, Bangalore. He had also served as the Secretary of the Board of Theological Education of the Senate of Serampore College}

■■■

FFRRC: Prospects and Challenges in its Mission and Vision

Fr. Dr. Jose John

Introduction

Federated Faculty for Research in Religion and Culture, one of the most prestigious theological institutions in Kerala under the Senate of Serampore system, was formally inaugurated on St. Thomas Day, July 3, 1980. On its Ruby Jubilee celebration I would like to greet all well-wishers and organizers of FFRRC and pray for successful academic pursuit and progress of FFRRC in its theological education. The FFRRC marked the beginning of a new ecumenical-theological research programme with the cooperation of three reputed theological seminaries in Kerala namely, Orthodox, Marthoma and CSI. I am proud to be a part of this esteemed institution and thank God Almighty for the successful growth and progress of FFRRC in these days. I would like to share some of my ideas regarding the prospects and challenges of FFRRC in its vision and mission while heading towards the Golden Jubilee Celebration which falls in the year 2030.

Mission and Vision of FFRRC

In the mission statement of FFRRC we read thus

> Federated Faculty for Research in Religion and Culture is an academic institution committed to promote theological, philosophical, hermeneutical, ecumenical discussions and discourses in order to disseminate epistemological and methodological innovations and mediations within the academia and among the faith communities, irrespective of caste, creed, confessions, ethnicity and gender distinctions and discriminations. FFRRC espouses a wider ecumenical vision rooted in the perichoretic understanding of Trinity revealed through the unfathomable love of Jesus Christ, the Word Incarnate. As a centre for higher theological learning, FFRRC envisions to creatively engage with the academia, both secular and theological, exemplifying the theologizing process in the Indian context, by entering into a dialogue with the religio-political, socio-cultural and ideological polyphonies and particularities, with a conscious commitment to the Triune God, to the world of God and to the people of God" (https://www.ots.edu.in/).

From the above passage we learn that FFRRC aims at the promotion of integrated theological research in an ecumenical perspective in the Indian context. Since we have crossed four decades in our theological journey, we need to have a self-evaluation of our vision and mission in the academic pursuit of the last forty years. Whether we could carry out the vision and mission of the pioneers is a very pertinent and significant question that we must analyze and evaluate. Moreover, in the present socio-cultural and theological scenario we have to decide what tools we need to adopt for the betterment of theological education in the Indian context.

Historical and Theological Analysis

Historically speaking, the FFRRC family could accomplish the mission and vision of its pioneers by producing able and competent academicians, theologians and Christian ministers of the day. It has been facilitating research in disciplines related to religion and culture, particularly theological disciplines leading to the master's and doctoral degrees of Serampore University as well as of other recognized universities/ research centres conforming to the goal of FFRRC. It is with a great sense of fulfilment and happiness that we recognize that many of the theological teachers and professors under the Senate system are the alumni of FFRRC. Thus, FFRRC has been able to achieve its vision to equip candidates for theological teaching and provide facilities for theological research in the Indian context. Moreover, it could also prepare theological teachers and academicians to actively engage in higher theological learning. With immense joy and pleasure, we realize the fact that FFRRC could equip candidates for various ministries in the Indian context. The FFRRC continues to promote in depth studies of Church traditions considering the secular, religious and the ecumenical contexts in India.

The promotion of mission studies and missionaries has been a central point of theological enterprise of FFRRC which was undertaken in order to strengthen the life of the churches to carry out its ministries in the pluralistic context of India. In earlier days the Indian Church was fully dependant on the western churches and missionaries for the mission enterprises in India. Western mission was replaced by indigenous mission endeavours through missiological and theological education. Today the Indian church is highly missiological in its perspective and engages in various mission activities with self-supporting and self-propagating consciousness and in accordance with the needs of the society. FFRRC played a major role in promoting mission studies and missionaries in the Indian context.

The COVID-19 pandemic has brought radical changes in the life and vision of the Church and society. It made possible virtual conferences both national and international. The pandemic period opened a new digital culture and consciousness among the populace. Even though the pre-pandemic period witnessed national or regional theological discussions in the FFRRC curriculum the pandemic period opened a new horizon of virtual discourses and learning. It made possible regular and consistent national and international conferences which in turn provided digital space and the opportunity to interact with eminent theological scholars and academicians. Participation in the webinars enhanced the e-learning culture among the research scholars. International and inter-religious dialogues were held occasionally which provided a forum for creative discussion and interaction between religious and secular scholars and among theologians in India. FFRRC is credited with the promotion of ecumenical co-operation and religious harmony through its educational mission.

In its theological journey over the last forty years, FFRRC could not take up seriously the non-degree research programme due to various reasons. It was the vision and mission of the FFRRC to engage with non-degree research programme to promote theological education on a wider perspective. FFRRC disregarded the non-degree research programmes knowingly or unknowingly in its academic pursuit. It is not known why the FFRRC overlooked the non-degree programmes. The systematic and sophisticated academic degree programmes might have hindered the gradual progression of the non-degree research programmes. It is the need of the hour to look into this matter seriously and make necessary arrangements for the more vibrant promotion of non-degree research programme to engage with common people.

In the post-epidemic era, we need to mould Christian leaders and ministers who are thoughtful and reflective in their attitudes towards the major or minor issues of our time drawing strength from the deep resources of faith. Our task is to mould the future ministers and leaders rooted in scripture, tradition, scholarship and religious harmony. In view of the Golden Jubilee celebration in 2030, we need to plan many things in relation to the vision and mission of the FFRRC to make it a unique theological educational institution in India. Following are some of the suggestions.

1. Centre of Academic Excellence

For the last forty years FFRRC has been rendering a remarkable contribution to the theological education in India. FFRRC had been founded on an excellent theological foundation with well-qualified theological scholars and academicians. It has been functioning as one of the best doctoral centers in South India par excellence. It is the duty and academic responsibility of the current academicians to strengthen the academic quality of the centre to train the future theologians of India. According to Aristotle, "Excellence is never an accident. It is always the result of high intention, sincere effort and intelligent execution; it represents the wise choice of many alternatives- choice, not chance, determines your destiny" (https:// www quotesgram.com). It is very clear from the above statement that if we want to maintain academic excellence, it will not happen accidently. It can be attained through high intention, sincere effort and intelligent execution. FFRRC needs to maintain its academic quality and its excellence. Therefore, high intention and sincere effort from our side is inevitable and we should execute the measures intelligibly to maintain the academic excellence that we received from our predecessors. It is our choice, and that choice will determine our future. While we celebrate the Ruby Jubilee of the FFRRC it is our task and mission to strive for the academic excellence of FFRRC for the benefit of the posterity. We need to study the possibilities of this mission and fulfill the criterion for the crystallization of this mission. As members of the academic faculty, it is our duty to provide the needed physical as well as digital facilities like e-library, smart classrooms and other research oriented services to enhance the quality of theological education and research programmes in FFRRC. New technologies and alternatives are to be explored for the betterment of the theological education in this digital era. Availability of online resources and digital library will surely promote and strengthen the theological education and research programmes. Therefore, we need to enhance our capacity to use new technologies and devices for our teaching ministry and research programmes. The quality of theological education should not be compromised at any cost.

We should continue our theological education with vigour and integrity in educating and forming Christian ministers and leaders for transformative leadership. Academic excellence should not be confined to academic matters only, but it should bring wholistic transformation of the person engaged in relation with the quality of life and Christian witness. Thus, by improving academic excellence we could transform the person/s and the community with which he is involved. A spirit of collegiality rather than competition in community life should be promoted along with the academic excellence which in turn will encourage religious harmony among communities. Collegiality could create an atmosphere of openness with all people irrespective of caste, colour and creed. When, for example, differences in theological positions, denominational affiliations or understandings of ministry occur, those differences should be expressed and addressed in a manner that respects each person's growth in wholeness and each person's gifts to the larger body (https://www.westernsem.edu).

Academic excellence and inquiry are essential to both research programmes and public ministry. Excellence involves the necessity of asking difficult questions, wrestling with controversial issues, and dedicating oneself to the disciplines of prayer, study, worship, research, dialogue and continuing growth. In the spirit of freedom and in dedication to the truth, some issues will be challenging for students, staff and faculty alike. The community values the opportunity to engage in dialogue, debate and inquiry at its very best without demeaning or devaluing another person in the process. Our pursuit of excellence should not be confused with perfectionism, which inevitably leads to loss of community with self and others. Instead, it should be understood as the worship of God with our minds and the proper stewardship of our intellectual gifts (https://www.westernsem.edu).

2. Ecumenical Centre for Christian Unity

FFRRC has been a centre for ecumenical friendship and academic fellowship to promote theological education in India since its inception. The different seminaries, belonging to different faith affirmation and confession, came together to begin a new journey of theological learning and education with commitment and academic passion in an ecumenical spirit. There were many practical hurdles and anxieties regarding the formation and development of this institution. By the grace of God Almighty and the ecumenical fellowship and fraternity of its member seminaries, FFRRC continues to stay united overcoming many theological as well as practical challenges in its growth. The academic fraternity and cooperation among the member churches and seminaries make FFRRC a unique centre of theological education in an ecumenical spirit. FFRRC promotes and stands for ecumenical unity and cooperation. The ecumenical spirit and passion for theological education in India has been fostered and promoted and needs to continue so for posterity too. Education will equip the person/s to 'understand the other' in a better way. Theological differences and doctrinal disparities can be understood and explained in an ecumenical spirit without hurting the other through theological education. An ecumenical theological perspective will foster ecumenical relationship and cooperation. FFRRC should maintain its ecumenical theological perspective and ecumenical spirit for the promotion of theological education in India for the benefit of Indian Christianity.

Ecumenical theological perspective should aim at the formation of individuals in the egalitarian concept where neither racial, creedal nor gender inequalities should be promoted. Christian ministers and leaders should be informed of the dangers of discrimination and divisions in the society due to the inequality and unequal proportions in the perspectives and attitudes. In Christ, divisions predicated on gender, race, or social status are put aside (Galatians 3:28). An individual is to reflect the reality that the dividing walls of hostility between people have been broken down by their being united in the body of Christ (Ephesians 2:13-16). Every effort should be made by the members of the FFRRC community to encourage and ensure such ecumenical unity.

As an ecumenical education centre, FFRRC should promote unity and collaboration among its member churches. In other words, it is called to deepen fellowship among its participants and broaden their participation, and facilitate greater coherence. Ecumenical dialogue can promote greater mutual understanding and intimate fellowship among different Christian traditions. According to Paulose Gregorios "Our ecumenism remains primarily a matter of policy and strategy of parrying and negotiating between Churches, of occasional sorties from our normal self-sufficiency to include the separated brethren in a charitable embrace soon to return to our own self-sufficiency" (Jacob Kurian ed., *On Ecumenism*, 3). And he adds,

> Ecumenism means heartfelt charity or love and respect towards adherents of other Christian Churches. It means refusal to caricature

> the faith and practices of the other even in private. It means a conscious effort to participate in other`s worship and thought. It means crossing the road to go to his Church occasionally, not out of curiosity, but genuinely participate in the other`s worship. It means creating an atmosphere in which we can speak to one another without fear of derision or contempt about the deeper realities of our faith, as we know them. It means struggling together to overcome our prejudices and to break through walls of separation built up over the years" (Jacob Kurian ed., *On Ecumenism*, 18).

Real ecumenical spirit and dynamism will promote and encourage fellowship and communion among us in all our ecumenical efforts and endeavours. Lack of ecumenical spirit and misunderstanding of the concept of ecumenism will weaken the fellowship and *koinonia* among members. Promotion of fellowship and *koinonia* alone can save and protect our humanity from the threats of socio-economic and religious-political issues of the new millennium. Therefore, as an ecumenical centre FFRRC needs to take into serious consideration Christian unity and cooperation and strive tirelessly to attain them. Ecumenism is not a matter of mere meeting together to engage in polite dialogue and then having a few programmes of common action. Ecumenism is the mission of God in our time –not only for the Church, but for the salvation of the world (Jacob Kurian ed., *On Ecumenism*, 244).

3. Centre of Letters

It must be noted that FFRRC was reluctant to produce theological literature/contribution in the last forty years of existence with just a few exceptions. It could have developed its own theological perspectives and perception through the publication of theological journals and periodicals. Each of the member seminaries and its faculty contribute to theological publication. But these contributions are individual and personal but the theological literary contribution of FFRRC as an institution is less significant, even insignificant. As a doctoral research centre for than four decades, FFRRC needs to take up the publication of theological journals or books as its mission. An earnest attempt should be made to publish theological books, journals and periodicals regularly. The Ruby Jubilee celebrations should be a signpost for the promotion of theological literature. Publication of theological literature will enhance theological education as well as research programmes.

The publication of theological literature will help to develop a special 'line of thought' in theological education. FFRRC as an ecumenical education centre needs to be 'inclusive' in its perspectives and perceptions. Converging methodology is commendable and advisable in an ecumenical circle. Different theological perceptions and perspectives need to be seen as different ways of interpreting the same topic/subject and should be encouraged. FFRRC should take theological literary publication as a challenge and strive to accomplish it at the earliest. Published materials become the historical documents for tomorrow's academic research. Literary contributions are inevitable and indispensable for research and academic pursuits. It is our duty and responsibility to make FFRRC a 'centre of letters' through the publication of theological books and journals, a treasure trove for posterity.

4. Centre for Wider Ecumenism and Inter-Religious Dialogue

As an ecumenical education centre, FFRRC should give primary importance to ecumenical and inter-religious relationships in the pluralistic context of India. In the earlier centuries, Indian Christianity was influenced by the multi-religious concept of India and each religion was considered a way of life towards the Supreme God. The influence of this multi-religious concept helped Indian Christianity to maintain religious harmony with other religious traditions in the Indian soil. This type of harmonious relationship between religious traditions is today termed as 'wider ecumenism', 'new ecumenism' and 'mega ecumenism'. Ecumenists are of the opinion that the term ecumenism should indeed deal with the plurality of the world as such, including its religious plurality. Religious plurality and the coexistence of different religious traditions is not a new idea or culture for Indians. But western colonization brought drastic changes in the mindset of Indians and gave rise to religious hatred and antagonism. Due to the impact of the ecumenical movement today there are inter-religious dialogues and co-operation between different religious traditions. However, the dangers of religious fundamentalism and religious hatred cannot be disregarded. Therefore, theological students need to be trained to discern the demands of the society and act according to the needs of the common people in their particular social contexts without losing either the Christian values or its ethos. Our future generations should not be narrow-minded or blinkered. On the other hand they need to broad-minded and armed with Christian values and ethics. Future theologians and Christian leaders should respect and revere the pluralistic context of India for the well being of all creation (www.westernsem https://.edu).

FFRRC has been promoting inter-religious dialogues and debates to enriching the mission and vision of its pioneers. The pluralistic context of India demand theologians and academicians with pluralistic perspectives and outlook. Inter-religious dialogues and debates are helpful methods for promoting religious harmony and synchronization. Religious fundamentalism and fanaticism are increasing day by day in the Indian sub-continent. Therefore, it is the need of the hour to have inter-religious dialogues to promote religious tolerance and harmonious life in today's Indian context. FFRRC, knowing its mission and vision, needs to conduct seminars and conference where students can come together to share their views and outlook thereby reducing religious antagonism and denominational hatred. Wider ecumenism and inter-religious dialogues need to be practised for the well being of all creation human and otherwise.

5. Centre of Linguistics

A linguist is one who studies the language. Linguists study every aspect of language including vocabulary, grammar, phonetics etc. The study of language is called linguistics and the people who study linguistics are called linguists. The study of linguistics is an indispensable factor that FFRRC needs to take up without much delay. As a doctoral centre which promotes biblical and patristic studies, a language institute is mandatory for the successful functioning of the research programme. Most of the faculty members are experts in language studies and therefore it would be quite easy for FFRRC to constitute a language institute where students from other theological institutions can also make use of this facility. The promotion of language studies will surely enrich research programmes and bring about theological advancement. Advanced studies of classical and modern languages will surely make FFRRC a unique centre of theological education and research programme in India.

Conclusion

As a research centre, FFRRC has been promoting admirable theological education and research programmes in its academic mission. For the last forty years it has been a model for ecumenical fraternity and theological collaboration amidst theological and doctrinal differences. It is a unique theological institution in India with its ecumenical spirit and theological cooperation. Heading to its Golden Jubilee, FFRRC needs to be more cautious about its duties and responsibilities in moulding future Christian ministers and leaders for India.

{Fr. Dr. Jose John, an ordained priest of the Malankara Orthodox Syrian Church, serving as a Professor and Research Guide in the department of History of Christianity at the Orthodox Theological Seminary and the Federated Faculty for Research in Religion and Culture, (FFRRC) Kottayam. He was the former Registrar of the FFRRC and the Orthodox Theological Seminary, Kottayam. He published many books and articles.}

■■■

Federated Faculty for Research in Religion and Culture:

A Brief Report

Rev. Dr. Koshy P. Varughese, Registrar

Mission Statement

Federated Faculty for Research in Religion and Culture (FFRRC) Kerala, is an academic institution committed to promote theological, philosophical, hermeneutical, ecumenical discussions and discourses to disseminate epistemological and methodological innovations and mediations within the academia and among the faith communities, irrespective of caste, creed, confession, ethnicity and gender distinctions and discriminations.

The Beginning

The Federated Faculty for Research in Religion and Culture in Kerala is a pioneering ecumenical venture among the theological fraternity under the Senate of Serampore College. FFRRC was founded as a joint programme of the Orthodox Theological Seminary, Kottayam, the Mar Thoma Theological Seminary, Kottayam and the Kerala United Theological Seminary, Thiruvananthapuram, and sponsored by the Orthodox Church, the Mar Thoma Church and the Dioceses of the Church of South India in Kerala.

In the mid 1970s, the theological fraternity in Kerala explored the possibility of setting up a post-graduate theological faculty in Kerala. The first meeting of an exploratory committee, consisting of delegates from the St. Thomas Apostolic Seminary (Vadavathoor), Mar Thoma Theological Seminary (Kottayam), Orthodox Theological Seminary (Kottayam), and Kerala United Theological Seminary (Trivandrum) was held at the Sophia Centre, Kottayam on July 30, 1977. Dr. T. V. Philip, then Director of the Senate also attended the deliberations. In 1979, a formal application for affiliation signed by Dr. Paulose Mar Gregorios (Principal, Orthodox Theological Seminary), Rev. Dr. V. P. Thomas (Principal, Mar Thoma Theological Seminary) and Rev. Dr. Jacob Verghese (Principal, Kerala United Theological Seminary) was submitted to the Registrar of the Senate of Serampore College. The Evaluation Commission appointed by the Committee on Academic Affairs visited the seminaries in November 1979 and submitted its report to the CAA. The Evaluation Commission Report was presented before the Senate meeting held on February 1, 1980, at Tamil Nadu Theological Seminary. The Senate of the Serampore College recognized FFRRC as a Post Graduate Centre for theological education and granted affiliation at the M. Th. level and permitted FFRRC to begin Master of Theology courses in the branches of Old Testament, New Testament and Christian Theology from the academic year 1980-81.

Inauguration of FFRRC

The FFRRC was formally inaugurated on July 3, 1980, St. Thomas Day. A meeting was conducted at the auditorium of Mar Thoma Seminary High School, Kottayam. Prof. Dr. Sukumar Azhikode, the pro-vice chancellor of Calicut University was the main speaker. A souvenir edited by Fr.Dr. K. M. George, a faculty member of the FFRRC, was published on the occasion. The meeting was attended by heads of churches, principals, faculty and students of federated colleges. FFRRC since then has been a bridge builder in engaging the academia with the life and ministry of the church. His Grace Dr. Paulose Mar Gregorios Metropolitan was the first Chairman along with Rev. Dr. V. P. Thomas and Rev. Dr. Jacob Verghese who served as Co-Chairmen and Rev. Dr. M. J. Joseph as the Registrar.

Milestones

In the academic year 1988-89, FFRRC began offering M.Th. degree course in History of Christianity and in 1997-98 in Religions. FFRRC introduced two other M.Th. courses, on Early Teachers of Faith (Patristic Studies) and Liturgical Theology within the branch of Christian Theology from the academic year 1999-2000. In the academic year 2004, FFRRC began M.Th. Pastoral Counselling and in 2014 Mission Studies. From 1986 FFRRC had been a doctoral centre until the formation of the South Asia Theological Research Institute (SATHRI) in 1989 which since then had been functioning as the only doctoral centre under Serampore University till the decision to reorganize SATHRI and restart regional centres for doctoral studies in 1999. The Senate of Serampore College which met on 5 February 1999 recognized FFRRC as a Regional Doctoral Centre under SATHRI and granted permission to begin doctoral programme in the branches of Old Testament, New Testament, Christian Theology and History of Christianity.

Inauguration of FFRRC as Regional Doctoral Centre

The inauguration of FFRRC as a regional doctoral centre was held on 14thJuly 1999 at the Orthodox Theological Seminary, Kottayam. Prof. Dr. K. Rajasekaran Pillai, the Vice Chancellor of Mahatma Gandhi University, Kottayam was the main speaker. His Holiness Baselios Mar Thoma Mathews II, Malankara Metropolitan and Catholicos of the East of Malankara Orthodox Syrian Church, His

Grace Dr.Philipose Mar Chrysostom, the officiating Metropolitan of the Mar Thoma Church, Most Rev.Dr. K.J. Samuel, Moderator of the Church of South India and His Grace Geevarghese Mar Osthathios Metropolitan blessed the occasion with their presence. The presence of heads of churches, principals, faculty and students of federated colleges made the occasion a memorable one. In 2010 the Senate of Serampore College granted permission to begin the D.Th. programme in Pastoral Counselling. FFRRC also provides the opportunity to undertake Non-Degree Research Programme and encourages scholars to enrol in this programme. The General Body of FFRRC which met on 30 June 1999 decided to start the Non-Degree Research Programme and encourage scholars to be enrolled in this programme.

Partnership with the Ecumenical Christian Centre, Bangalore

The long-term association with ECC goes back to the period when Rev. Dr. M.J. Joseph was the director of ECC. The three-day academic programme at ECC is an annual feature of ECC and FFRRC. The theme for discussion each year is based on contemporary issues, methodological issues in Biblical hermeneutics etc. The faculty and students stay at the ECC campus and enjoy the hospitality of the ECC which arranges the resource persons for the programme. Students and faculty thus get an opportunity to interact with theologians and scholars from secular fields. Thanks to the directors Rev. Dr. M. J. Joseph, Rev. Dr. Mani Chacko,Rev.Dr. Cherian Thomas, Rev. Dr. Mathew Chandrakunnel and associate directors and office staff.

Association with the St. Thomas Apostolic Seminary, Vadavathoor, Kottayam

FFRRC builds up its theological fraternity with the faculty of St. Thomas Apostolic Seminary and *Paurasthya Vidya Peetom*,

Vadavathoor, Kottayam. The research scholars of FFRRC use faculty resources and library resources at Apostolic Seminary and *Paurasthya Vidya Peetom*. The faculty of FFRRC and *Paurasthy Vidya Peetom* occasionally meet and discuss theological issues to strengthen our ecumenical journey in building up future theological educators and church leaders for the church at large.

Silver Jubilee Celebrations

The 25th year Silver Jubilee Celebration of FFRRC was held in the year 2005 at the Orthodox Theological Seminary, Kottayam. His Grace the late Bishop Geevarghese Mar Athanasius of the Mar Thoma Church was the main speaker.

Colloquium and Seminars

FFRRC is always proud of its faculty members for their contributions to the theological field and to the Church as leaders in building the body of Christ. FFRRC is keen to arrange faculty colloquium. In addition to faculty members, we invite overseas theologians as well as scholars from secular fields. Seminars by students are one of the key academic endeavours in the life of FFRRC. Students present theological papers addressing contextual realities. This is an opportunity for students to get peer review for their findings, and for academic scrutiny by professors and scholars from the respective areas. Good number of presentations are being thus published in theological journals.

Alumni of FFRRC

FFRRC has around 468 M. Th graduates and 132 doctoral graduates till date. FFRRC is proud to say that a good number of theological teachers now serving at different seminaries in India and even abroad are alumni of FFRRC. A number of church leaders are also graduates of FFRRC.

Exposure Programme

We have long term association with premier theological institutions in Europe and United States. We are grateful to Missions Akademie Hamburg, Princeton Theological Seminary, New Jersey, U.S.A, Lutheran Theological Seminary, Chicago for their support in providing academic and research exposure to our students.

Ruby Year Celebrations

FFRRC celebrated the 40th year of its existence on 15th December 2021 at the Mar Thoma Theological Seminary Chapel. His Holiness Baselios Mar Thoma Mathews III, Malankara Metropolitan and Catholicos of the East of Malankara Orthodox Syrian Church, inaugurated the function. His Grace the Most Rev. Dr. Theodosius Mar Thoma the Metropolitan of the Malankara Mar Thoma Syrian Church gave the keynote address. His Grace the Most Rev. A. Dharmaraj Rasalam, the Moderator of the Church of South India, was the guest of honour. Rev.Dr. M. J. Joseph, the first Registrar of FFRRC, Rev.Dr. Zacharias Kannyakonil, Rector of Vadavathoor Apostolic Seminary, Rev.Dr. John Paniker P. L, the former Registrar, Rt.Rev.Dr. Royce Manoj Victor, a former faculty member and Dr. Jayasree K.B, an alumnus of FFRRC felicitated the occasion. A Ruby year commemorative volume edited by Fr. Dr. Jose John was released by His Grace Dr. Zacharias Mar Aprem, the President of the Senate of Serampore College. In appreciation of their contributions to the FFRRC, mementos were presented to the former and present faculty members. The presence of Heads of the Churches, the former and present faculty members and the students made the Ruby year celebration a memorable one.

Administrative Office and Hostels

The administrative office of FFRRC functions in the campus of the Mar Thoma Theological seminary, Kottayam. The Mar Thoma

Theological Seminary has set apart office facilities in the new administrative block free of cost for the FFRRC office. The FFRRC is grateful to the Mar Thoma Church and Mar Thoma Theological Seminary for providing office rooms and to Orthodox Theological Seminary for providing space for various meetings and seminars. We are thankful to Mar Thoma Seminary, Orthodox Theological Seminary and Kerala United Theological Seminary for providing hostel rooms and library facilities for our students.

Thanks

FFRRC is grateful to the three constituent churches, the Malankara Orthodox Syrian Church, the Mar Thoma Syrian Church and the Church of South India and the Governing Boards of three seminaries for the constant support extended to the activities of the FFRRC. We owe a debt of gratitude to the Senate of Serampore College, especially we gratefully acknowledge the Master of Serampore College, the presidents, registrars, the Deans of Research(SATHRI), the secretaries of BTESSC and the Academic Council and the Research Committee of the Senate for their timely advice and support. We acknowledge the generous support of the churches of India by sending their students to FFRRC for the higher level of learning thereby inculcating the spirit of ecumenism in them. FFRRC is indebted to the pioneers, former faculty members, present faculty members and alumni for building FFRRC into a centre of excellence.

FRRC continues its academic journey as an ecumenical platform to provide facilities for theological education leading to post graduate and doctoral degrees and also for non-degree research programs all across India. We humble ourselves before God Almighty for his faithfulness and guidance over the last forty years.

Your hand, O God, has guided your flock from age to age, your faithfulness is written on history's open page. Our fathers and mothers owned your goodness and we their deeds record; and both to this bear witness: one church, one faith, one Lord (adapted from E. H. Plumptre, Psalter Hymnal Handbook, 1988).

■■■

Faculty List

Present Office Bearers

Chairperson	Fr. Dr. Reji Mathew
Co-chairperson	Rev. Dr. V. S. Varghese
	Rev. Dr. C. I. David Joy
Registrar	Rev. Dr. Koshy P. Varughese
Treasurer	Rev. Dr. L. V. Bipinlal

Dean of Studies

D. Th. Fr. Dr. Ninan K. George

M. Th. Rev. Dr. Joseph Daniel

Heads of Department

Fr. Dr. Jacob Mathew (Old Testament)

Rev. Dr. Reji Mathew (New Testament)

Rev. Dr. John Philip A (Christian Theology)

Fr. Dr. Jose John (History of Christianity)

Fr. Dr. Shaji P. John (Christian Ministry)

Rev. Dr. M. T. Cherian (Religions).

Internal Auditor

Fr. Dr. Saji Varghese Amayil

Office Staff

Mrs. Darly George (Office secretary)

Current Faculty Members

Rev. Dr. Abraham Scaria P

Fr. Dr. Bijesh Philip

Rev. Dr. L. V. Bipin Lal

Rev. Dr. M. T. Cherian

Rev. Dr. C. I. David Joy

Fr. Dr. Filix Yohannan

Fr. Dr. Jacob Mathew

Rev. Dr. Joe Joseph Kuruvilla

Rev. Dr. John Philip A

Fr. Dr. John Thomas Karingattil

Fr. Dr. Jose John

Rev. Dr. Joseph Daniel

Rev. Dr. Koshy P. Varughese

Rev. Dr. Mothy Varkey

Fr. Dr. Ninan K. George

Fr. Dr. Regi Geevarghese

Fr. Dr. Reji Mathew

Fr. Dr. Saji Varghese Amayil

Fr. Dr. Shaji P. John

Rev. Dr. M. C. Thomas

Rev. Dr. V. S. Varghese

Visiting Professors

Rev. Dr. Abraham Philip

Fr. Dr. Baby Varghese

H. H. Dr. Baselios Mar Thoma Mathews III Metropolitan

H. G. Dr. Geevarghese Mar Yulios Metropolitan

Fr. Dr. K. M. George

Rev. Dr. Jacob Cherian

Rev. Dr. M. P. Joseph

Rev. Dr. Prakash K. George

Fr. Dr. O. Thomas

Fr. Dr. T. I. Varghese

Rev. Dr. Y.T. Vinayaraj

H. G. Dr. Zacharias Mar Aprem Metropolitan

Former Chairmen and co-chairmen

H.G. Dr. Paulos Mar Gregorios Metropolitan

Rev. Dr. V. P. Thomas

Rev. Dr. Jacob Verghese

Rev. Dr. K. C. Mathew

Rev. Dr. K. V. Mathew

Rev. Dr. M. J. Joseph

Rev. Dr K. M. George

Rev. Dr. M. V. Abraham

Most. Rev. Dr. J. W. Gladstone

Rev. Dr. K. K. Koshy

Rev. Dr. K. P. Kuruvilla

Rev. Dr. Kuruvilla George

Rev. Dr. P.S. Daniel

Rev. Dr. T. P. Abraham

Rev. Dr. Abraham Kuruvilla

Rev. Dr. Geevarghese Mathew

Very Rev. Dr. K. G. Pothen

Rev. Dr. G. Shobhanam

Rev. Dr. D. Burnabas

Rev. Dr. P. T. George

Fr. Dr. Jacob Kurien

Fr. Dr. O. Thomas

Rev. Dr. M. P. Joseph

Rev. Dr. Prakash K. George

Fr. Dr. Johns Abraham Konat

Rev. Dr. C. I. David Joy

Former Registrars

Rev. Dr. M. J. Joseph

Fr. Dr. V. P. Varghese

Rt. Rev. Dr. J. W. Gladstone

Rev. Dr. K. V. Mathew

Rev. Dr. Cherian Thomas

H.G. Dr. Gabriel Mar Gregorios Metropolitan

Rev. Dr. John Paniker

H.G. Dr. Yuhanon Mar Demetrios Metropolitan

Very Rev. Dr. K. G. Pothen

Fr. Dr. Reji Mathew

Rev. Dr. V. S. Varghese

Fr. Dr. Jose John

Former Treasurers

Rev. Dr. K. P. Kuruvilla

Rev. Dr. G. Shobanam

Rev. Dr. D. Burnabas

Rev. Dr. M. P. Joseph

Rev. Dr. John Winslow

Former Dean of Studies (D. Th)

Rev. Dr. T. P. Abraham

Rev. Dr. Geevarghese Mathew

H.G. Dr. Yuhanon Mar Demetrios Metropolitan

Rt. Rev. Dr. Mathews Mar Makarios

Rev.Fr. Dr. Baby Varghese

Rev. Dr. Abraham Philip

Fr. Dr. Reji Mathew

Rev. Fr. Dr. Jose John

Rev. Dr. V. S. Varghese

Former Dean of Studies (M. Th)

Rev. Fr. Dr. T. I. Varghese

Rev. Dr. Abraham Philip

H.G. Dr. Mathews Mar Thimothios Metropolitan

Rev. Dr. K. A. Abraham

Rev.Fr. Dr. Jose John

Rev. Dr. Sunni E. Mathew

Rev.Fr. Dr. Ninan K. George

Former Faculty Members

Rev. Dr. K. A. Abraham

Rev. Dr. Abraham Kuruvilla

Rev. Dr. M. V. Abraham

Rev. Dr. Abraham Philip

Rev. Dr. Abraham Stephen

Rev. Dr. T. P. Abraham

Rev. Dr. Alex Thomas

Rev. Dr. D. Burnabas

Rev. Dr. K. K. Cherian

Very. Rev. Dr. Cherian Thomas
Rev. Dr. P.S. Daniel
H.G. Dr. Gabriel Mar Gregorios Metropolitan
Rev. Dr. K. A. George
Prof. Dr. K. C. George
Fr. Dr. K. M. George
Rev. Dr. P. G. George
Rev. Dr. P. T. George
Rev. Dr. Jacob Cherian
Fr. Dr. Jacob Kurien
Rev. Dr. Jacob Thomas T.
Rev. Dr. Jacob Verghese
Fr. Dr. M. O. John
Rev. Dr. P. L. John Paniker.
Rev. Dr. John Winslow
Fr. Dr. Johns Abraham Konat
Rev. Dr. M. J. Joseph
Rev. Dr. M. P. Joseph
Prof. Dr. Joseph P. Varghese
Rev. Dr. K. K. Koshy
Rev. Dr. Kuruvilla George
Rt. Rev. Dr. K. P. Kuruvilla
Prof. P. K. Mathai
Rev. Dr. K. V. Mathew
Rt. Rev. Dr. Mathews Mar Makarios
H.G. Dr. Mathews Mar Thimothios Metropolitan
H.G. Dr. Paulos Mar Gregorios Metropolitan
Very. Rev. Dr. K. G. Pothen
Rev. Dr. Prakash K. George

Rev. Dr. Prinstone Ben
Rt. Rev. Dr. Royce Manoj Victor
Rev. Dr. Sabu Philip
Rev. Dr. G. Shobanam
Rev. Dr. Sunni E. Mathew
Prof. Dr. Susan John
Fr. Dr. O. Thomas
Rev. Dr. R. C. Thomas
Prof. Thomas Thomas
Fr. Dr. T. I. Varghese
Fr. Dr. V. P. Varghese
H.G. Dr. Yuhanon Mar Demetrios Metropolitan
H.G. Dr. Yuhanon Mar Diascoros Metropolitan
H.G. Dr. Zacharias Mar Aprem Metropolitan

■■■

www.ingramcontent.com/pod-product-compliance
Ingram Content Group UK Ltd.
Pitfield, Milton Keynes, MK11 3LW, UK
UKHW041827200726
13854UKWH00002BA/611

9 789390 569281